PRAISE FOR *FOR THE LOVE OF MARY*

"Erudite, pious, orthodox, and readable, *For the Love of Mary* is a fantastic book on Our Lady! The Franciscans have always had a tremendous devotion to Mary, and Fr. Klimek proves himself a true son of St. Francis by continuing to teach, preach, and write about the titles, privileges, and wonders of the Mother of God. Everyone who reads this book will find their hearts expanding and their minds contemplating the greatness of the Immaculata. I very highly recommend this book!"

FR. DONALD CALLOWAY, M.I.C.
Author of Consecration to St. Joseph

"Fr. Klimek has given a valuable gift to us with this beautiful book. He has provided us with what we need to find a 'path of love' with Our Lady, the Mother of God. In moving vignettes, Fr. Klimek tells us of several saints—from St. Louis de Montfort to St. Maximilian Maria Kolbe to St. John Paul II—who credit the presence of Mary in their lives as key to their path of sanctification in Christ. Filled with moving stories, *For the Love of Mary* will inspire readers to develop or deepen their own loving relationship with Mary by inviting her into their inner lives."

ANNE HENDERSHOTT
Director of the Veritas Center for Ethics in Public Life at Franciscan University of Steubenville and Author of The Politics of Envy

"If, as the author says early in this book, the mystic is one who not only loves but falls in love with God, then this book is the writing of a mystic. Fr. Klimek graces us by sharing a most intimately personal love of his Mother Mary. His love in relationship with her radiates through these pages in which we do not simply hear about our Mother. We meet her; we relate to her. Especially valuable is his treatment of the sorrowful Mother and her share in the passion of her Son—indeed her stigmata."

FR. THOMAS ACKLIN, O.S.B.
Professor of Theology, Saint Vincent Seminary,
and Coauthor of Spiritual Direction *and* Personal Prayer

"I found *For the Love of Mary* most edifying and nourishing of my faith and love of the triune God, of Jesus Christ, and of my heavenly Mother. Readers will appreciate the many beautiful quotes from Saints Bernardino, Maximilian Kolbe, Bonaventure, Catherine of Siena, Francis, John Paul II, and Faustina, as well as descriptions of their relevant works on Mary. The breadth and depth of the book and the constant impression on the reader that the author is indeed 'in love' with our heavenly mother Mary make this book a very, very special one. I recommend it enthusiastically and without reservation."

JOSEF SEIFERT
Philosopher and Founder of the John Paul II
Academy for Human Life and Family

"*For the Love of Mary* beckons the reader to a deeper relationship with the Blessed Mother. In it we encounter Mary's maternal and feminine qualities, reflect on her sufferings, and feel her comfort. Fr. Klimek masterfully elucidates, too, Mary as warrior, fighting for her son. He guides us on a journey of encounter with Mary through the saints, mystics, and her various apparitions throughout the world. At its core, this readable work reminds us, 'Saying Yes to Beloved Mary means saying Yes to Jesus.' It is readily evident how Fr. Klimek's personal love for Mother Mary helped him to produce this fine work as a labor of love for the Church."

VERY REV. MALACHI VAN TASSELL, T.O.R.
President, Saint Francis University

For the
LOVE OF MARY

For the
LOVE OF MARY

FR. DANIEL-MARIA KLIMEK, T.O.R.

EMMAUS
ROAD
PUBLISHING

Steubenville, Ohio
www.emmausroad.org

EMMAUS
ROAD

Emmaus Road Publishing
1468 Parkview Circle
Steubenville, Ohio 43952

Library of Congress Control Number 2022936864
ISBN 978-1-64585-242-1 (Hardcover) |978-1-64585-243-8 (Paperback) |
978-1-64585-244-5 (Ebook)

Cover design and layout by Allison Merrick
Cover Image: *Madonna and Child* by Giovanni Battista Salvi, 1640.

*This book is dedicated to my best friend since childhood,
someone who has been by my side even before I knew it,
who has watched over me, protected me, and guided me
toward finding meaning, love, and my priestly vocation:
my beloved Mother and dearest friend,
the Blessed Virgin Mary.*

*I would also like to dedicate this book to Cindy Costello,
Ginna Dombrowski, and Brenda Lombardi, beautiful souls who
have allowed me to experience, in one way or another,
the maternal face of Mary through their spiritual friendship.*

With gratitude and love.

CONTENTS

I am in love with the Most Blessed Virgin, Mother of God. I have always loved her. I have a burning desire to see her; I love her with all my heart, and so I have chosen her as my most chaste betrothed. I would like to keep my gaze fixed on her constantly, and that is why I decided to visit her every day.

—*St. Bernardine of Siena*

ACKNOWLEDGEMENTS

While writing this book, I spent ten days in Poland, revisiting the beautiful city of my childhood, Kraków. I am immensely thankful to my cousin, Anna Drożdżak, who allowed me to stay in an unoccupied family apartment and provided the gracious hospitality and resources that I needed to turn the apartment into a writer's haven for that period. When I was not writing, Anna took me around Kraków Old Town, showing me the beauty of the medieval city and, through her example and radiant goodness, showing me the gift of family and friendship. During this time, we visited Lipnica Murowana, a small village in southern Poland from which my father's family originates. Memories of praying together before the tombstone of our grandparents and aunts, with Anna and her brother Szymon, on a cool, breezy, and colorful October afternoon come back to me fondly.

I am immensely thankful to James Merrick for first proposing this book project to me. Knowing James has been a gift, and I am grateful that friendship could lead to various professional collaborations.

Thank you to Dr. Josef Seifert and Jakub Dudek for very helpful suggestions to the manuscript which have improved the quality of the final product.

Jennifer Holmstrom has offered me some of the deepest theological and spiritual conversations I have ever encountered. Jennie's insights have contributed to my knowledge of nuances of Marian devotion which have benefited a chapter in this book.

I am grateful to Samantha Oswald for research assistance on the major Marian apparitions. Her work was comprehensive.

Working with the editorial staff of Emmaus Road Publishing has been a joy. Thank you especially to Chris Erickson, Melissa Girard, Madeleine Cook, and all those who contributed to the manuscript. Madeleine was the first person to read my manuscript and offer feedback. Her heartfelt words of support meant more to me than I can express, and I am deeply thankful for Madeleine's impeccable editing of the book.

My colleague at Franciscan University of Steubenville, Mark Miravalle, who has been teaching Mariology at the university since 1986—the year that I was born!—has contributed more than anyone to my knowledge of Mariology and Marian spirituality through his writings, books, and lectures. Mark's wisdom permeates many pages of this book. Before I knew him as a colleague, I knew him as an intellectual hero, wholly devoted to our Holy Mother.

I am incredibly grateful to Scott Hahn for the support and friendship that he has shown me over the past years. Since I was a young deacon, preaching my first masses in Steubenville, Scott has been a constant presence of moral support, encouragement, and a witness to faith. It is a privilege to have Scott read this work, and how appropriate that when it came down to choosing the right title for the book, it was Scott who came up with the perfect one.

My appreciation to Fr. Brian Cavanaugh, T.O.R., for words of encouragement and motivation when I needed to hear them about this project.

My appreciation to those friends and family members who have offered prayers and sacrifices during the writing of this book. And, finally, I would like to thank the faculty, students, and staff of Franciscan University of Steubenville, both in Ohio and at the study abroad campus in Austria, for all their support. They are a family of faith and scholarship, with whom it has been an honor to share this journey.

INTRODUCTION

We need to fall in love with Our Lady, with beloved Mary. It is that simple. It is what Jesus desires. It is His will, a reality that would give Him great joy.

The epigraph that begins this book speaks to the heart of this reality. St. Bernardine of Siena, the great late-medieval Franciscan preacher, reformer, and mystic, confided these impassioned words to his cousin Tobia. In Siena, outside one of the northern portals in the medieval walls of the city, the Porta Camollia, there was a fresco portraying Our Lady's Assumption into heaven, an artwork that spoke to Bernardine deeply and that he visited frequently as a youth, spending much time in prayer before the sacred image of the Madonna.[1] The daily effort of offering loving prayers before the Blessed Virgin's image was seen by Bernardine as a daily visitation with her.

Bernardine's words speak to a deeper love. Bernardine was a mystic. Mystics are individuals who do not simply love God but who are *in love* with God. There is a difference. There is a depth and single-minded radicality, an all-or-nothing fervor and interior devotion. It is no accident that two of the greatest texts of the Bible which many Christian mystics throughout history have connected with most are the Song of Songs and the Gospel of John. The Song of Songs, that radiant Old Testament love story portraying the soul's relationship with God as a love affair, an intimate relationship between the soul and the Beloved, who is Christ. And the Gospel of John, written by the "beloved disciple," the true mystic among Jesus's followers, whose words soar like

---

[1] As cited in Luigi Gambero, *Mary in the Middle Ages: The Blessed Virgin Mary in the Thought of Medieval Latin Theologians* (San Francisco: Ignatius Press, 2005), 290.

an eagle's wings onto sublime heights of contemplation because he had a deeper, more interior and spiritual communion with Jesus, understanding Him in His poignant dignity and sacred divinity—a knowledge that is experiential, and therefore of a higher nature, because it comes from the soul of a contemplative in love with the Lord.

It is also possible to reach similar heights of love with Our Lady, the Mother of God. There are many who do not simply love her but, reflective of St. Bernardine's impassioned words, are absolutely in love with her. "Marian souls," as St. Louis de Montfort famously called such fervent devotees. While many people do love Mother Mary immensely, there are many others, however, who do not love her or do not know how to love her, desiring a more intimate relationship and not being sure how to get there in their spiritual lives.

That is what this book is about: the path of love with Mother Mary.

How do we fall in love with Our Lady? How do we spiritually foster and cultivate this important relationship to help us reach a more intimate union with her, the mother of Jesus? There are numerous ways, which this work will delve into in detail.

We need, first and foremost, to walk with her and speak to her daily, choosing to live with the presence of Mary in our lives. We need to see her for who she is: a close, affectionate mother who desires our good, who ceaselessly prays and intercedes for us before the throne of God as our advocate, and who has been present throughout our lives, even when we did not know it, in an invisible and yet tenderly felt way. We need to listen to her voice and hear her messages by reading about her major apparitions, the times that God has allowed her to visit the human race in a more personal, supernatural manner in order to deliver messages from heaven, to call us on to lives of prayer, conversion, and sacrifice, and lead us away from sin and toward the divine Light that is her Son, Jesus.

We need to spiritually unite our sufferings with her sufferings, making it a regular practice to meet her at the foot of the Cross, allowing her to fulfill the role in our lives by which one beautiful Marian title invokes her name, Comforter of the Afflicted. We will look at her role as Mother of Sorrows, and how important it is to cultivate devotion to her in that sacred identity. It's an opportunity for us to unite ourselves with Jesus and Mary through the intimacy of suffering. We are called to share in their honor, but that also means that we cannot avoid sharing in their dishonor as well, in the betrayal and pain that they have experienced and which life often brings us—it is a painful intimacy, bittersweet, yet there is a beauty in it, the beauty of sharing in their hurt. Life is full of joys, glories, and sorrows, the mysteries of the Rosary become a reflection of our own experiences, and when we unite those difficult experiences with the sorrows of Jesus and Mary, they are transformed, leading to intimacy and intercession.

This book will offer insights into Mother Mary's sufferings that are seldom realized. Among those sufferings, we will consider the possibility, present in the Catholic mystical tradition and supported by a strong theological basis, that she was the first stigmatic, experiencing the interior holocaust of Christ's wounds invisibly in her body during His Passion. We will also explore how, in addition to her wonderfully maternal and feminine nature, Our Lady—predating a St. Joan of Arc—is a warrior. She is the Woman who does battle with the dragon and who calls us to lives that are part of a cosmic adventure and battle; she calls us on to be knights, maidens, and soldiers for the Queen of Heaven, in union with St. Michael and the heavenly armies, the angels and saints, fighting against the forces of darkness in a spiritual war that has eternal consequences and can be responsible for the salvation of countless souls, our own included. We will consider not only the biblical and theological basis for this reality but also the testimonies of exorcists who have personally witnessed the power of the Mother of God in the midst of spiritual battle against demons.

She figures prominently in the Rite of Exorcism, new and old, and has a central place in the spiritual war that cannot be ignored if one truly wants to understand her sacred influence and identity. A Yes to Our Lady, when we give her our *fiat*—which is essentially an invitation from God, since Jesus desires us to have an intimate relationship with His Mother, ordaining this reality from the Cross when, as His final act on earth, He proclaimed, "Behold, your mother!" (John 19:27)—is a response that will lead to a life of deep meaning, spiritual engagement, and loving communion with the Woman who was Jesus's best friend when He walked the earth and continues to sit beside Him in heaven as the Queen Mother. She desires our friendship and intimacy. She desires to be the Mother in our lives who will offer consolation, comfort in times of sorrow and pain, a loving, joyful presence to speak to and contemplate as we share our blessings, struggles, and daily endeavors with her.

Saying Yes to beloved Mary means saying Yes to Jesus. A relationship with her never takes away from a relationship with Him but, in fact, honors Him and strengthens the relationship. A person comes to love Him through her. For to honor the Mother is to honor the Son. And, therefore, as the medieval Cistercian monk St. Aelred articulated, "We owe her honor, for she is the mother of our Lord. He who fails to honor the mother clearly dishonors the son. Also, Scripture says: 'Honor your father and your mother.'"[2]

This book is meant to invite you on a spiritual journey of tender love, a journey that calls you to better know, honor, and come to love our precious heavenly Mother. Knowing her better and loving her leads to a deeper spirituality, to a life of holiness and

---

[2] St. Aelred, Sermon 20, in *Nativitate beatiae Mariae*: PL 195, 322–324. Quoted in *The Liturgy of the Hours*, vol. 4, *Ordinary Time* (New York: Catholic Book Publishing, 1975), 1637.

happiness that places Jesus at the center in a special way, through the loving hands of the living tabernacle that is His Mother.

Know that if you are reading this book, it is because something drew you to it—or better yet, someone. Our Lady desires your intimacy and affection. As the Spiritual Mother of the human race, she plays a role in your life, and you have a place in her heart. Knowing and loving her better never takes away from Jesus but enriches one's spiritual life with a deeper love for Him, as a person becomes immensely grateful to the Lord for His generosity in allowing a soul to have a relationship with such a sweet, maternal presence, with beloved Mary.

May you approach this work prayerfully, may it bless you with spiritual riches, and may you open your heart to the grace that the Holy Spirit desires to work within you through a sacred relationship with His spouse. If you already have that Marian relationship, may this book help deepen it in areas of understanding and intimacy. If you do not, may that relationship be pursued, and I hope that this book can provide the inspiration for that life-transforming pursuit.

Fr. Daniel-Maria Klimek, T.O.R.
December 27, 2021
Steubenville, Ohio
Feast of St. John, Apostle and Evangelist

Chapter 1

WHAT'S IN A NAME?

Terms of Endearment

Of all prayers to the Blessed Virgin the shortest and, in a certain sense, the most perfect is the invocation of the name of Mary—or its equivalent, "Mother." . . . These holy names [of Jesus and Mary] may take on a long litany of meanings, depending on your state of soul and on our needs of the moment. "Mary!" sometimes means "I love you, Mother!" Sometimes it means "Help me," or "Thanks," or "For you," or "In your name"; at other times, "I am sorrowful, console me," or "I have sinned, obtain pardon of Jesus for me," and so on.

—Fr. Emile Neubert

This may sound strange. In fact, often when I give a talk or homily about Our Lady and I mention this fact, it initially surprises, even scandalizes, people for the first few moments. I can see the bewildered expressions before I explain what I mean.

It is this: I don't particularly like to use the name "Mary" or even refer to Our Lady by her name—by *simply* her name, that is. And I mean that with the utmost respect, as Our Lady's name is beautiful and, behind the name of Jesus, is the most sacred name in the world, easily the most sacred feminine name that exists. Let me explain further.

When I entered the novitiate, the second year of religious life in our Franciscan order, when you receive the habit and officially become a religious, I had the option of changing my name, or adding to it, with a religious name. This process included writing a letter to our superiors explaining why we wanted religious names, for those of us who prayerfully discerned that the Lord was calling us to request a different name. After much thought, prayer, and consideration, my request became not to fully change my name but to add to it.

To my baptismal name of Daniel I desired to add the name "Maria." In my letter, I also requested that the two names be connected by a hyphen, hence, becoming a Franciscan friar, I would be known as Brother Daniel-Maria (before, years later, becoming "Father").

I was overjoyed when the request was granted, a reality that was personally made known to us in front of our families during a public liturgical ceremony where we received our Franciscan habits, the ancient garments of St. Francis of Assisi, along with a white cord symbolizing the vows of poverty, chastity, and obedience, as Francis and his early followers wore.

There is an ancient tradition in Christianity, very prominent in the medieval period, of men and women in religious life adding the name "Mary," or some variation of it, to their first name. While I was grateful to inherit and walk in this ancient, reverent practice honoring our Blessed Mother, it was not the tradition itself that was my primary reason for adding her name. It was my personal experience with her, the fact that Our Lady has been instrumental in my spiritual journey and life.

It was because of her that I experienced a life-transforming conversion through which I was led to an intimate relationship with Jesus, which altered the course of my life. And it was through her intercession that I felt the calling to religious life and the priesthood, which has given my life deep meaning and purpose in serving the Kingdom of God for the salvation of souls. She has always been there, and she will always continue to guide me, as long as I am faithful to the relationship.

Thus, adding her name was an act of love and reverence, but

also a reminder to me. It was a reminder of the person who has been there for me from the beginning, and who continues to lead me to holiness; the mother and beloved friend who reminds me who I am, a son of Mary, and therefore a brother of Jesus. The hyphen between the two names was important for me because it signified a unity and closeness that my life, in its Marian devotion, must aspire to in order to stay pure. I have noticed early on that the holiest priests I've known have usually been men who have been very close to Our Lady, she being their secret to holiness. I knew that if I were to live that life of holiness as a religious and eventually a priest, particularly during a time when there is so much need (and, sadly, so little expression) of holiness in the priesthood, I needed to stay close to her.

Hence, what's in a name? Everything. Memory, identity, mission, hope, purpose, path. And the name of "Maria," as I desired to have it in its ancient Latin expression, is sacred. Fr. Jacques Philippe writes similarly about the biblical significance of one's name, especially as it originates from the father in the biblical tradition. "The father helps his child find his or her true identity. In the Bible, the father gives the child its name. The name is not just a label, a word to be called by, but it represents a deep identity, the mission of the person."[1]

There have been different interpretations by scholars about the original meaning of the name *Mary*, an ancient name that has interestingly been difficult to delineate, leading to countless etymologies and discussions, stemming from both Hebrew and Egyptian origins. Three prominent interpretations of the name of Mary include "Light-giver," "beloved of God," and "rebellion."[2]

---

[1] Jacques Philippe, *Priestly Fatherhood: Treasure in Earthen Vessels* (New York: Scepter Publishers, 2021), 23.

[2] For an insightful discussion of the etymologies, history, and the present complexities in delineating the name of Mary, see Richard Kugelman, "The Holy Name of Mary," in *Mariology*, ed. Juniper B. Carol, O.F.M (Post Falls, ID: Mediatrix Press, 2018), 1:439–52.

If a name speaks to a person's identity and mission, the first expression, Light-giver, has twofold significance: it signifies Mary's role as the one who brings Christ, the true Light, into the world, and it also denotes her role in the realm of spiritual warfare—a topic we shall discuss in detail in a subsequent chapter—specifically in countering the great enemy of Christ and the human race, Lucifer, whose name means "Light-Bearer."

Whereas the title "beloved of God" may make perfect sense, the other one mentioned, "rebellion" or "to rebel," may particularly strike readers as strange or unfitting. That is, even if it is etymologically and philologically accurate—in this case, "Mary" being derived from the Hebrew word מְרִי (which is transliterated *meri*, meaning "rebellion")—the thought may be that the word certainly does not signify the sacred mission or identity of the person of Mary. Her fiat, after all, constitutes absolute opposition to Satan's rebellion, her yes to serve God counters Satan's no. That revered fiat, therefore, becomes an act of radical loyalty toward the divine order, a defense of the sacred against the chaos that Satan and his fallen angels introduced.

In fact, it is probable that the definition or meaning of "rebellion" was not considered or intended by parents in ancient Near Eastern or Middle Eastern cultures when choosing to name their daughter Mary—that is, some variation of the name. As mentioned, the name of a child in the biblical tradition was deeply rooted in the identity and mission of the child. Therefore, the word "rebellion," a term that connotes a revolt against a righteous authority, including God and his law, would not make sense for a young girl, especially in the Jewish tradition. The word *Satan*, whose name actually denotes "adversary" or "opposition" perfectly fits the arch-*rebel* who wanted to be like God, as if he could dethrone the Almighty in his rebellion.

The name *Maria* or *Mariam*, in New Testament Greek transliterated to Μαριάμ, derives from the Hebrew *Miryam*, most famously identified in the Old Testament in the sister of Moses. *Miryam*, however, may be derived from *marah* or from *mara*. Whereas the former means "to be rebellious," the latter means "to be well nourished."[3] The latter would make greater sense in the naming of a daughter since ancient Eastern cultures associated being well-nourished with beauty and bodily perfection—in this sense, "Mary" would be identified as the beautiful and perfect one.[4] Theologically, this would make further sense because Our Lady is the only creature, since Adam and Eve, to have a soul that is "full of grace"—thus, that is substantially nourished by God's grace! Every other person has been deprived of that fullness of grace that was originally intended for our souls but which sin has taken from us. On the level of grace, no creature was as well-nourished as she was.

Other meanings associated with the name of Mary, which are quite fitting when considering her identity and mission, have included "hope," "strong one," "ruling one," "great sorrow," "healed one," "gracious one," "exalted one," and "star of the sea."[5] The latter title, from the Latin *stella maris*, especially becomes a beautiful symbol of Our Lady as a shining light that protects and guides us amongst the stormy waves that the sea of life offers.

If there is so much beauty, meaning, and owed reverence present in Our Lady's name, and if her name means so much to me that I have united it to my own in order to make up my religious identity, then why do I tell people that I do not like to use the name "Mary" in reference to her?

It is simple. What I am getting at is this: Would you ever call your mother by her first name?

No, of course not.

That would seem distant, informal, and strange—a bit too

---

3 "The Name of Mary," *Catholic Encyclopedia*, https://www.newadvent.org/cathen/15464a.htm.

4 "The Name of Mary," *Catholic Encyclopedia*.

5 "The Name of Mary," *Catholic Encyclopedia*.

avant-garde, to be sure! Instead, you would use terms of endearment and familiarity.

Although it is not always an exact science, sometimes you are able to detect how close, or how distant, a person's relationship to Our Lady is on the basis of *how* they refer to her. Quite frequently, a person who does not know Our Lady closely can be inclined toward referring to her simply by her first name in their speech, making reference to "Mary" as if referring to a distant, historical figure of the past. However, it is fascinating to hear how differently those who have a close relationship with Our Lady often address her.

St. Maximilian Kolbe, one of the great Marian devotees of the twentieth century (or, for that matter, of any century), often referred to Our Lady as "Mom."

How appropriate and endearing!

Whether it is Mom, Mama Mary, Mother Mary, Our Lady, Our Holy Mother, Blessed Mary, or Beloved Mary, you can often tell the degree of affection that a person has toward our Spiritual Mother by how lovingly they address her.

What about visionaries who have seen Our Lady, who have had apparitions of her maternal presence? Do they address her simply by her first name?

Usually not, as they sense the depths of her maternal love and use words of deep affection, intimacy, and closeness. A wonderful example of this comes from the young Marian visionaries of Kibeho, Rwanda, who began experiencing apparitions of Our Lady as teenagers in 1981. Kibeho would eventually become the first Marian apparition site on the African continent to receive Church approval.

The first visionary of Kibeho, Alphonsine Mumureke, surprised many people when, during her apparitions and afterward, they heard her address Our Lady as "my dear," "my darling," and "Mom."[6]

At first, the people of Kibeho and visiting pilgrims were bewildered, even a bit scandalized, by how such terms of affectionate endearment could be used with the Mother of God, expecting a more formal address. But as the visionaries have pointed out, she is first and foremost their mom, who loves them dearly. Therefore, they speak so affectionately to her as a sign of the deepest, most heartfelt and loving respect toward Our Lady.

"She loves us—that's what I feel the most when she's with me," Alphonsine has said.[7] When asked how she could use such personal terms of endearment with the Virgin Mary, Alphonsine replied, "Because she wants us to talk to her like she's our mom, not like she's our principal or boss."[8]

And that's absolutely key. *She wants us to talk to her like she's our mom.*

Sometimes the deepest truths about spirituality are expressed not by the most brilliant theologians but by the simplest souls, their simplicity and humility disposing them toward holiness and the truths of holiness. In this case, Alphonsine teaches us, through Our Lady's wisdom, an important dimension of prayer to our Holy Mother. It should be a prayer of the heart that addresses her as a mom. We need to learn to speak to her, to address her from the most inner depths of our hearts, as our own loving mother. For that is who she is in the order of grace.[9]

If you are not used to using such affectionate language with

---

[6] See Immaculée Ilibagiza, *Our Lady of Kibeho: Mary Speaks to the World from the Heart of Africa* (New York: Hayhouse Inc., 2008), 131–32.

[7] Ilibagiza, *Our Lady of Kibeho*, 41.

[8] Ilibagiza, *Our Lady of Kibeho*, 44.

[9] See also: "This maternity of Mary in the order of grace began with the consent which she gave in faith at the Annunciation and which she sustained without wavering beneath the cross, and lasts until the eternal fulfillment of all the elect." Second Vatican Council, *Lumen Gentium* (1964), §62.

Mother Mary in your prayer, I simply encourage you to start. It will help change your prayer and your relationship with her.

Sometimes when I speak to her, from my heart, the words just take off: "beloved," "my love," "beautiful and sweet Maria." They are not only the words of a son toward his Spiritual Mother but also the gentle words of the Spirit who lives and prays within me, through my baptism, speaking to His beloved spouse.

Our Lady desires your intimacy. Do not hesitate to call her by a more tender and sensitive expression of loving admiration, because if you knew how much she loved you, you would cry from joy.

Marian visionaries have often acknowledged this fact, that when they are in her presence, it is the depths of her motherly love that overwhelm them—a love so deep that it is incomparable to any human love they have ever felt or known, even that of the best earthly mothers.

"Her love is so powerful," Alphonsine has said, "that it could lift you up and carry you to heaven. When I see her, I can't see anything else; the rest of the world disappears, and there's just the lady and her beautiful light. Imagine how much your mom loves you, and then multiply that love a million times. . . . The lady loves us even a million times more than that."[10]

Let us respond to that love. We begin with language. Prayer usually starts verbally and mentally before it becomes more silent and contemplative. Let us begin to speak to her from the heart, sharing with our beautiful mom our various emotions and experiences—the joys, fears, struggles, blessings that surround us. And let us refer to her in intimate ways. The language that we use will help shape the affections of our prayer. If you struggle with feeling affection for our beautiful mom, then just begin by calling her "Mom" each day, or a similar term of endearment, and speak to her from your heart. Enter this daily, loving practice. She desires your intimacy and affection. Do not be afraid to tenderly express it.

---

[10] Ilibagiza, *Our Lady of Kibeho*, 41.

Chapter 2

A ROSE OF WONDROUS BEAUTY

The rosary is the weapon that wins all battles.
—*St. Padre Pio of Pietrelcina*

I myself have often encouraged the frequent recitation of the Rosary. From my youthful years this prayer has held an important place in my spiritual life. . . . The Rosary has accompanied me in moments of joy and in moments of difficulty. To it I have entrusted any number of concerns; in it I have always found comfort.
—*Pope St. John Paul II*

It was late, about 10:30 PM. A seminarian at the time in Washington, DC, I was still up.

A text message came.

It was like hearing from a ghost.

A friend whom I had not heard from in a very long time had sent an urgent message asking for help. The text asked for prayers, explaining that his girlfriend was pregnant and wanted to have an abortion.

This was incredibly heavy, I thought. And it was just beginning.

Moments later another text came. It explained that his girlfriend was planning to get the abortion *tomorrow*, again pleading for help.

I showed the texts to one of my brother friars. He encouraged me to communicate to my friend how he needed to do everything he possibly could to talk his girlfriend out of it, to persuade her that this could not be the right choice. It was true, and my friend on the other side of that text—who is pro-life and wanted nothing to do with abortion—had already been trying, pleading with her to no avail.

When human persuasion does not work, more needs to be done, especially in terms of imploring the power of God's grace. Prayer needs to be our foundation—and sometimes, even more than prayer, genuine sacrifice. Oftentimes the strongest acts of intercession come from sacrifice: something that is difficult and demanding and truly resembles Jesus taking up the Cross.

I realized then that if his girlfriend was planning to get the abortion in the morning, I needed to spend this night in prayer, offer the sacrifice of the night. How often did Jesus spend the night in prayer before a significant event the following day? The Lord teaches us a way—*the Way*—by His example.

I started praying in my room, and very quickly something significant came to my mind in the midst of prayer. The thought came: *this is a spiritual battle.*

It is a spiritual battle for the life of this child.

Satan and his demons rejoice at the horrific sin and tragedy of abortion—in a very real way, it is a child sacrifice to the evil one—and at that time they were winning the battle over this young woman's mind, using all their resources. In that moment I realized that I needed to use all of the spiritual resources at my disposal to fight for this child's life.

In other words, it couldn't just be my prayer and my sacrifice of the night. If Satan was using his demons, his forces of darkness, I needed to turn to spiritual warriors of the light. I decided that night to send out a number of emails and text messages to some of the most prayerful people I have ever met with this intention, including priests who would be able to offer Mass for the intention. It can be humbling, contacting people—many of whom you haven't been in touch with in years—for help. But that's exactly what my friend was doing with me, and I needed to swallow my pride and do the same by passing along this urgent intention at this late hour.

Not only did I decide that night to contact people I knew, but I also asked favors from friends who had influential online Catholic media followings, that they spread the intention and ask their faithful followers to pray that this young woman would choose life for her child. I worded the intention in a way that explained the situation without betraying the identity of the person involved.

Among the people I contacted, I sent the intention to my friends Denis and Cathy Nolan, a married couple who run the media station *Mary TV*, which reports events from the Marian pilgrimage site of Medjugorje. Each morning, as they have done for years, Denis and Cathy pray a Rosary, streaming it live as they pray with thousands of their viewers. They took the intention to heart, announcing it on air and having their viewers join in offering their Rosaries in praying for this mother and the life of her unborn child.

It is probable that we had tens of thousands of people praying for the intention. It made me think of a beautiful line from one of the recent *Star Wars* films: "Darkness rises, and the Light to meet it."[1]

Satan was bringing his forces. We responded by turning to his archrival, the most holy Virgin Mary, the true Light-bearer. The Mother of God, hearing thousands of souls praying, brought the intention before her Son, and what happened next I will never forget.

My friend and I spoke over the phone two days later. It was going to be a difficult conversation, I knew, and I wasn't sure whether I was ready for it. What he said, however, absolutely astounded me.

He told me that he couldn't believe what had happened. His

---

[1] *Star Wars: The Last Jedi*, directed by Rian Johnson (San Francisco, CA: Lucasfilm Ltd., 2017), DVD.

girlfriend had woken up that morning—the morning that she was planning to get the abortion—and it was as if she were a completely different person. She no longer wanted the abortion! In fact, she found out that day that the baby was going to be a girl. What a remarkable gift! What a miracle! I thought. *Praised be Jesus and Mary!*

A child saved from the darkness of death.

When my friend found out how many people were praying for his daughter, and especially going to Our Lady's intercession by taking up the rosary, he decided upon her birth to give his daughter the middle name *Rosario*.

To this day, when I think of that dear child, I refer to her in my mind as Rosario, knowing that she is a daughter of Mary in a very special way who was saved by the intercession of her heavenly Mother and the powerful spiritual weapon that is the Rosary.

I thank the Lord Jesus and Mother Mary for this work of grace.

Let us consider in greater detail the power and depths of the Rosary, as it is a form of prayer that is especially dear to Mother Mary—how often has she appeared with the rosary in her hands and urged the faithful to pray with her during her major apparitions. At the same time, the Rosary is a devotion that many people struggle with or do not fully appreciate, often finding the repetition of Hail Marys to be dry and mechanical. Let us consider ways to delve deeper with the Rosary, in order for it to truly become a meditative prayer of the heart.

Meditating on Our Lady's Memories

One of the greatest writings on the Rosary ever published—which everyone who wants to delve deeper with this devotion should read—is Pope St. John Paul II's apostolic letter *Rosarium Virginis Mariae*. This work is really a masterpiece of spirituality and prayer. It is also the work that formally gave us the Luminous

Mysteries of the Rosary, which were introduced by the Polish pontiff in 2002.

In this work, St. John Paul II also gives us remarkable insights about the proper spiritual dynamics that are in play in praying the Rosary. He writes:

> In a unique way the face of the Son belongs to Mary. It was in her womb that Christ was formed, receiving from her a human resemblance which points to an even greater spiritual closeness. No one has ever devoted himself to the contemplation of the face of Christ as faithfully as Mary. . . . Mary lived with her eyes fixed on Christ, treasuring his every word: "She kept all these things, pondering them in her heart" (*Lk* 2:19; cf. 2:51). The memories of Jesus, impressed upon her heart, were always with her, leading her to reflect on the various moments of her life at her Son's side. In a way those memories were to be the "rosary" which she recited uninterruptedly throughout her earthly life.[2]

This paragraph alone possesses so much spiritual food! Beginning with the closeness of Jesus and Mary, St. John Paul II speaks about a reality that we perhaps seldom think about: there would be a human resemblance between the two, between the face of Jesus and the face of Mary, as she gave birth to Him and provided Him with His sacred flesh. Looking at her, one would be able to see the Son, and the resemblance would be mutual: as Jesus grew, friends and relatives would be able to recognize His mother's face in His as well.

This tender resemblance points to the even greater one of spiritual likeness and closeness between the two. St. John Paul II rightly stresses that no one contemplated the face of Christ as

---

[2] John Paul II, Apostolic Letter *Rosarium Virginis Mariae* (2002), §§10–11.

intimately as Mary, and that she treasured in her heart the memories that she held of her Jesus. It is those memories which she meditated upon throughout her life and which became the Rosary. This is a profound insight that should deeply affect the way that we pray the Rosary.

St. John Paul II once wrote that praying the Rosary well required entering a proper psychological state, a psychology of love.[3] In other words, it is a mindset of an affectionate encounter, realizing that the Rosary is not just verbal repetition but a loving encounter with a real person. This especially becomes the reality when we recognize that to pray the Rosary well means being in the presence of Mother Mary and contemplating her memories. However, this psychological dynamic proper to love is ultimately directed toward Jesus, whose life constitutes Our Lady's memories. Thus we contemplate and love Him "with her and through her."[4] This insight and understanding of St. John Paul II brings a meaningful dimension to grasping the sacred encounter that is the Rosary.

Think about it. There is a beautiful woman filled with unspeakable maternal love for you who wants to meet with you every day. One day she is going to share with you some of the happiest memories of her life, times of pure joy, such as when her precious child was born and the wonders that were prophesied about His life. Another day she is going to share with you some of the saddest memories of her life, moments of excruciating suffering, such as when her child was killed in front of her. Another day she is going to share with you some of the most luminous and glorious memories of her life, moments when she experienced the miracles and the mystical amazements of God in a special way.

---

[3] John Paul II wrote: "To understand the Rosary, one has to enter into the psychological dynamic proper to love." Quoted in Marianne Lorraine Trouvé, FSP, ed., *John Paul II: A Marian Treasury* (Boston, MA: Pauline Books and Media, 2005), 136.

[4] John Paul II, quoted in Trouvé, *A Marian Treasury*, 136.

She is sharing her life story with you, sharing her testimony. It takes so much trust and vulnerability for a person to share in this way, to share so openly. It speaks of profound intimacy between persons who are able to encounter each other with such depth. It speaks of the intimacy that Our Lady wants with us and is calling us to.

St. John Paul II said that every day he schedules a meeting with her, the Mother of God. We need to see the daily encounter of the Rosary in a similar light. It is not the rote repetition of mechanical prayers—even if sometimes it can feel that way—but no, at its heart, the Rosary is a daily encounter with Mother Mary, who wants to share with us the deepest memories of her heart, which are a meditation on the life of her beloved Jesus, as she always points to her Son. And in that encounter, she mediates our intentions before the throne of God and we can also pray for her intentions, the various intentions that her heart holds for the world, having a mutually giving and beautifully loving relationship with her.

The mysteries of the Rosary are, of course, a meditation on the life of Jesus. They are also Our Lady's memories, as she was there for so many events in the life of Christ, to whom no one was closer than she. The first mystery of the Rosary, the Annunciation, begins with her, and the last mystery of the Rosary, the Coronation in Heaven, ends with her. But all of these mysteries do not stop with her but point to Him, as that is the center of her life and mission, bringing others closer to her Son. She will use her memories and the intimacy of that daily encounter that we can have with her to bring us closer to Jesus. As St. John Paul II artfully explained, "To recite the Rosary is nothing other than to *contemplate with Mary the face of Christ*."[5]

There is a charming and very meaningful story that St. Louis

---

[5] John Paul II, *Rosarium Virginis Mariae*, §3.

de Montfort shares in his classic work *Secrets of the Rosary*. It is an episode from the life of another holy man. St. Louis writes:

> The life of Blessed Hermann (of the Premonstratensian Fathers) tells us that one time when he used to say the Rosary attentively and devoutly while meditating upon the mysteries Our Lady used to appear to him resplendent in breathtaking majesty and beauty. But as time went on his fervor cooled and he fell into the way of saying his Rosary hurriedly and without giving it his full attention. Then one day Our Lady appeared to him again—only this time she was far from beautiful and her face was furrowed and drawn with sadness. Blessed Hermann was appalled at the change in her, and then Our Lady explained:
>
> "This is how I look to you, Hermann, because in your soul this is how you are treating me; as a woman to be despised and of no importance. Why do you no longer greet me with respect and attention meditating on my mysteries and praising my privileges?"[6]

This is a deeply meaningful story because it shows us how our devotion to the Rosary speaks to an actual encounter and relationship with a real woman. And the way that we approach the prayer of the Rosary speaks volumes toward how we are treating her and whether we are honoring her in this relationship.

Essentially, Our Lady wants to bring us to a deeper, contemplative way of praying, where we truly meditate on the mysteries and internalize the sacred words of the Rosary with our hearts—not just rushing through them with lip service. This is not to say

---

[6] St. Louis de Montfort, *The Secret of the Rosary* (Charlotte, NC: TAN Books, 1987), 104.

that sometimes the Rosary won't feel difficult and mechanical, even if we're making a sincere effort. It certainly can and will, as there are periods when prayer, in general, can become dry and feel mechanical. In those periods, it is important not to give up on prayer but to keep persevering and to realize what prayer is in its essence: it is an act of love. And love is especially tried and proven to be true when it is acted on without the benefit of consolations. In those moments, therefore, when dryness is present, we can especially show Our Lady how much we love her by being true to the devotion that is so close to her heart even when our own hearts lack consolation. Frequently, even if we do not feel consolations during the prayer, we do experience the fruits of the prayer soon after or even the next day, as there is great grace that the meaningful praying of the Rosary brings. The fruit of prayer is virtue, becoming more Christlike and allowing that intimate transformation that the Lord works interiorly to touch others as well. Sometimes, God is a pragmatist. It's not about feelings but about interior union and transforming fruits.

There is a wonderful story of Bishop Fulton Sheen instructing a woman who came to him and proclaimed that she would never become a Catholic, arguing against the faith by using the Rosary in her reasoning. The woman explained that the Rosary is filled with repetition, repetition of the same words and prayers, and that those who simply repeat the same words are never sincere and should not be believed, by others or by God. Bishop Sheen noticed that she came with a man and asked who he was. She replied that he was her fiancé.

Bishop Sheen asked, "Does he love you?"

"Certainly, he does," she replied.

"But how do you know?"

"He told me."

"What did he say?"

"He said: 'I love you.'"

"When did he tell you last?"

"About an hour ago."

"Did he tell you before?"

"Yes, last night. He tells me every night."

"Don't believe him," Bishop Sheen concluded. "He is repeating; he is not sincere."[7]

This pastorally graceful encounter on Bishop Sheen's part tells us another secret about the Rosary. The repetition is part of cultivating a loving relationship.

Each day there is an opportunity to renew our love in the relationship. This should be perceived not as a burden but as a gift. The perpetual repetition of Our Fathers and Hail Marys and Glory Bes are daily acts of affection and renewed love for the most Holy Trinity and the Blessed Virgin Mary. Authentic love is not proven by an occasional act of goodness but by long-term and constant affection that requires repetition and daily, caring sacrifices. Frequently, the greatest sacrifice that we have to offer is our time.

Often a person will say that they do not have time to pray the Rosary each day; life is too busy. But the truth is, we always make time for the things that we love and that are important to us. It is not time that we lack. It is love.

Repetition also has the power of helping us enter into a more contemplative, loving disposition, wherein we slowly start to become one with a spirit of prayer. It becomes second nature to us. No longer difficult or mechanical, but part of our breathing, the prayer enters our interior. Fr. Thomas Acklin and Fr. Boniface Hicks articulate this reality beautifully in their book *Personal Prayer*:

---

[7] This dialogue is cited from one of the best books written about the Rosary in recent years. See Fr. Donald H. Calloway, MIC, *Champions of the Rosary: The History and Heroes of a Spiritual Weapon* (Stockbridge, MA: Marian Press, 2016), 309.

Repetition also helps us to detach from the words and helps make the words a part of us so that they flow out of our breath and heartbeat. Our prayer becomes more apophatic, letting go of images and stimulating only an affection of the heart or a willed adherence to the Lord. We find ourselves simply carried into the Heart of Christ through the Heart of Mary.[8]

Offering Her a Spiritual Bouquet

Every Hail Mary prayed sincerely is a rose that is being offered to her, our Spiritual Mother. Every rose is a display of affection and love. This is not just a figure of speech but speaks to the reality of a spiritual bouquet that can be offered as a daily gift to our Mother. There is a significant late-medieval story, prominent in the Franciscan tradition, which popularized the word "rosary" and truly revealed an important glimpse of what the devotion entails in terms of intimately offering Our Lady a bouquet of spiritual roses. St. Maximilian Kolbe loved telling the story to his friars.

It happened in 1422. There was a young Franciscan novice named James who, when he was a lay person, had the custom of bringing roses and placing them before an image of the Madonna. However, after James entered religious life, he was no longer allowed to perform this act of love each day. He was, in fact, contemplating leaving religious life for this reason.

Until it happened.

He had a mystical experience of Our Lady that not only saved his vocation but also gave us a profound insight into the spiritual depths and dynamics of the Rosary. St. Maximilian explains, telling the story:

---

[8] Fr. Thomas Acklin, OSB, and Fr. Boniface Hicks, OSB, *Personal Prayer: A Guide for Receiving the Father's Love* (Steubenville, OH: Emmaus Road, 2019), 248.

While he was afflicted in this way, the Blessed Virgin Mary appeared to him and said: "Recite devoutly my psalter, and adorn me with the most beautiful flowers." He began therefore to pray the rosary, and immediately he saw how for each Hail Mary the Blessed Virgin Mary took forth from his mouth a rose of wondrous beauty and weaved with those roses a garland for herself. At the Our Father she wove into the garland a resplendent lily. This was the origin of the name "Rosary."[9]

This encounter is significant for a few reasons.

First, it reiterates the point that to pray the Rosary is to experience an *encounter* with the Virgin Mary. The Rosary constitutes a spirituality of encounter. That is why St. John Paul II was right in referring to his daily time of praying the Rosary as a scheduled meeting with a person. It is noteworthy also that when Our Lady gave the Fatima visionary Sr. Lucia dos Santos the First Five Saturdays devotion, one of the requests that she made was to "keep me company" while meditating on the mysteries of the Rosary.[10] In other words, Our Lady was directly explaining that when we meditate on the mysteries of the Rosary, she is there with us; we are keeping her company: the prayer of the Rosary is an invitation, a welcoming of her presence, and we have the sacred privilege of having that time with her. She is there, praying with us, contemplating the mysteries of the life of Christ with us, as she is sharing her memories of those mysteries. It is a beautifully intimate moment.

Second, the most important gift that we can offer Our Lady is our prayers. Notice how each Hail Mary, in this prominent visionary experience, was a "rose of wondrous beauty" offered to her; each Our Father a "resplendent lily." This experience was

---

[9] Quoted in Calloway, *Champions*, 40.
[10] We will look at the importance of this devotion in greater detail in chapter 6.

pivotal, Fr. Donald Calloway emphasizes, because it revealed that "all rosaries are ways of *crowning* Mary with spiritual roses."[11] He goes on to quote Pope Leo XIII, who in his encyclical *Parta Humano Generi*, wrote: "For as often as we greet Mary with the Angelic Salutation, 'full of grace,' we present to the Blessed Virgin, in the repetition of our words of praise, roses which emit the most delightful perfume."[12]

The prayers that we offer Our Lady are immensely important, and she takes so much joy in them, because not only are they acts of love but they also assist her, as the mediatrix of graces, to help distribute the graces that Jesus Christ merited on the Cross throughout the world. This is key: with our prayers of the Rosary, not only are we loving her and, through her, Jesus in offering her spiritual flowers and intimately meditating on her memories, the mysteries of the life of her Son, but we are also helping her fulfill the important mission of her Son: the salvation of souls, through the graces that will touch innumerable human beings in the world by the way that the Lord desires to use our prayers.

Third, the 1422 apparition is also important for giving us a new devotion known as the Franciscan Crown Rosary. With the visionary experience, Our Lady gave the Franciscan novice a new, seven-decade rosary that is dedicated to the "Joys of Mary." This Franciscan Crown Rosary added two new mysteries that constitute Mary's joys alongside five mysteries that are present in the traditional Rosary. Thus the "Joys of Mary," as expressed in the Franciscan Crown, include the Annunciation, the Visitation, the Nativity, the Adoration of the Magi, the Finding of the Child Jesus in the Temple, the Resurrection Appearance of Jesus to Mary, and the Assumption and Coronation of Our Lady, which in the Franciscan Crown Rosary are combined as one Joyful Mystery, the final one.

---

[11] Calloway, *Champions*, 41.
[12] Calloway, *Champions*, 41.

There is an ancient Christian tradition, prominent in medieval devotional belief, that the Lord's first Resurrection appearance was to His mother, Mary. It is a tradition that is supported by the revelations and writings of a number of mystics, in addition to the mystical revelation that produced the Franciscan Crown. Even Pope St. John Paul II, in his spiritual intuition, has expressed belief in such an account, explaining in a homily, "The gospels do not tell us of an appearance of the risen Christ to Mary. Nevertheless, as she was in a special way close to the Cross of her Son, she also had to have a privileged experience of his Resurrection."[13]

The Franciscan Crown Rosary, having seven decades instead of five, contains seventy Hail Marys in those decades, and two more are added at the end to make up seventy-two Hail Marys in total. This, likewise, pertains to a pious tradition, an ancient belief that Our Lady lived on the earth for seventy-two years before her Assumption.

A Contemplative Prayer

St. John Paul II explained that to enter the depths of the Rosary, the devotion needs to be prayed with a contemplative pace and disposition. It really needs to become an interior prayer of the heart, guided by Our Lady's sweet hand. The Rosary, "precisely because it starts with Mary's own experience, is *an exquisitely contemplative prayer*. Without this contemplative dimension, it would lose its meaning," he emphasized, pointing to Pope St. Paul VI's warning: "Without contemplation, the Rosary is a body without a soul, and its recitation runs the risk of becoming a mechanical repetition of formulas, in violation of the admonition of Christ: 'In praying do

---

[13] As cited in Msgr. Arthur Burton Calkins, "Mary: Co-redemptrix: The Beloved Associate of Christ," in *Mariology: A Guide for Priests, Deacons, Seminarians, and Consecrated Persons*, ed. Mark Miravalle (Goleta, CA: Seat of Wisdom Books, 2007), 397.

not heap up empty phrases as the Gentiles do; for they think they will be heard for their many words' (*Mt* 6:7)."[14]

St. John Paul II, therefore, gives us guidance on how the Rosary should be prayed to cultivate its contemplative dimensions. Again, he looks to the wisdom of Paul VI, who accentuated that by its very nature, the recitation of the Rosary "calls for a quiet rhythm and a lingering pace, helping the individual to meditate on the mysteries of the Lord's life as seen through the eyes of her who was closest to the Lord. In this way the unfathomable riches of these mysteries are disclosed."[15]

Notice the importance here of "a quiet rhythm and a lingering pace." This is an internal disposition that is essential to cultivating a contemplative prayer of the heart, which saves the Rosary from simply becoming lip service, something that needs to "get done," so to speak. We can, quite often, fall into this temptation of making the Rosary part of a daily "to-do list," going through the motions of mechanically (and, at times, superficially) reciting it. The popes recommend something else, a deeper experience of prayer.

A quiet rhythm and a lingering pace are fostered by regularly making intentional time for silence and solitude. Whether it is finding a church, a chapel, or entering the silence of one's room, the external environment can have a great influence on creating the right internal environment, the disposition of the soul that is conducive to stillness and contemplation. Not everyone, of course, has the luxury of finding a quiet environment in their daily life—I say this as someone who grew up in the noisy, urban atmosphere that is Chicago and a small, humble family home where too often it seemed impossible to find moments of privacy. It frequently meant seeking out distant churches, in the midst of the noise of the city, where quiet chapels of adoration were available, and with

---

[14] John Paul II, *Rosarium Virginis Mariae*, §12.
[15] John Paul II, *Rosarium Virginis Mariae*, §12.

them the opportunity to spiritually exhale and rest in the presence of the Lord.

When those opportunities are not available, it is still important to try to cultivate a prayerful quietness in the interior chapel of one's soul by making other sacrifices: whether it is waking up earlier or going to sleep later, there are hours where even the noisiest environments, be it home or the dormitory at school, experience stillness. Be it in the coming of the dawn or in the dark-lit tranquility of night, the opportunities to be "alone" with God and His Mother are available if we are willing to make loving sacrifices. Cardinal Robert Sarah writes:

> Christ often recommends that we withdraw if we want to pray. It may be a remote place, in solitude, so as to be alone with the Alone. But the question of the external setting cannot avoid the problem of interiority. It is important to create the interior room where man finds God in a genuine face-to-face encounter. This spiritual work demands effort in order to avoid all distraction, which presupposes interior asceticism. The search for interior silence is a path to perfection that demands repeated attempts.[16]

Sacrifice and asceticism are required to enter and cultivate that interior silence of the soul, repeated efforts of self-denial that lead to mastery. These loving sacrifices to increase one's communion with God are Christlike, as the Gospels show us the example of Jesus, who often sought places of silence and solitude to pray to the Father, even if it meant sacrificing rest during uncomfortable hours as the Apostles and the world around Him slept. Christ

---

[16] Robert Cardinal Sarah with Nicolas Diat, *The Power of Silence: Against the Dictatorship of Noise*, trans. Michael J. Miller (San Francisco: Ignatius Press, 2007), 55–56.

is our example of heroic virtue, and His life challenges us to ever-deeper sanctity, and there is no genuine sanctity without the Cross.

A "quiet rhythm and lingering pace" also draw us to the necessity of meditation. The Rosary is a prayer that is both verbal and mental. In addition to fostering an interior stillness of mind that tries to transcend distractions, we need to mindfully meditate on the mysteries that we are contemplating. There are different schools of Christian meditation, expressions that range from the Benedictine form of *lectio divina* to Franciscan and Ignatian models that strongly highlight the use of visual imagination, particularly using the imagination to place oneself into the Gospel scene that one is meditating upon and becoming immersed in the drama of the scene.[17]

For our purposes, we shall keep this simple by emphasizing that meditation on the Rosary can be divided into two major categories, either visual or discursive meditation. The type of meditation that appeals to a person is usually based on the individual's mental disposition: certain people are more visual while others are more discursive; yet others may be comfortable finding an integrated balance between the visual and discursive.

For the visual person, it may be easier to imagine a Gospel scene, one of the mysteries of the Rosary, vividly, and even to try to mentally place oneself into the scene: imaging, if they are contemplating the last Sorrowful Mystery, the blood dripping from the Cross, Jesus's exhausted and scarred face, the mocking shouts and blasphemies of the crowd, the sorrowful Mother in unbearable anguish supported by John and the Magdalene in a trauma that seems beyond her strength.

For the more discursive person, on the other hand, it may be

---

[17] A helpful scholarly book in understanding the prominent usage of imagination in medieval culture and meditative techniques is the work by Michelle Karnes, *Imagination, Meditation, and Cognition in the Middle Ages* (Chicago, IL: University of Chicago Press, 2011).

challenging to create a vivid mental picture with the imagination. Such a person may be more inclined toward meditating on language in their prayer over images. This could be the language of the prayers themselves, whether the Our Father or Hail Mary or Glory Be—thus the person may meditate on the words, "forgive us our trespasses as we forgive those who have trespassed against us," connecting them to Jesus's cry at the Crucifixion. Or the person may meditate on the language itself that is spoken in the mystery that is being meditated upon. Therefore, if the mystery is the Crucifixion, then the person may meditate on the words spoken by Jesus from the Cross, whether they are the words addressed to the good thief, or to John, or to Mother Mary, or to God the Father, when in His excruciating agony the Lord cried out, "My God, my God, why have you forsaken me?" (Matt 27:46).

Personally Entering the Prayer

What is especially spiritually fruitful, and thus very important—this is the case whether one is a visual or discursive person—is to take the meditation of the mysteries deeper to the next level by asking the self-reflective question, "How does this meditation pertain to my life?" or "What can it teach me?" Spirituality is meant to be self-implicating; it is not simply about the past but also about how the past reaches your present.

Perhaps you are going through an immense suffering in your life, feeling alone and abandoned by the heaviness of the trial; and contemplating the vulnerability and absolute poverty of Jesus on the Cross offers you some comfort, knowing that you are not alone in your pain and that, united with His Passion, your suffering can have redemptive value as an act of intercession for sinners. Perhaps you are someone who experienced the tragedy of losing a beloved family member and in the midst of that inconsolable grief, contemplating the suffering of Mother Mary at the foot of the Cross offers you spiritual intimacy, even the painful intimacy of suffering with her. You feel closer to her and the Crucified Christ than you ever had before, realizing that the interior sorrow that your heart is experiencing is increasing your intimacy with Calvary and leading to your sanctification. Perhaps you are in a state of mortal sin, desperately seeking reconciliation with God, and meditating on the Lord Jesus's compassionate words toward the good thief gives you hope, an interior experience of His Divine Mercy. Perhaps you are in a place in your life where you are experiencing deep loneliness, and the words that Jesus speaks to John from the Cross resonate with you like never before: "Behold, your mother" (John 19:27). You feel her closeness in the most personal way, an intimacy that is made more real by the interior pain that she is consoling in that moment, through her maternal presence, as you pray the Rosary *with her*, being engulfed under the consoling mantle of her Immaculate Heart as you feel your spirit flooded with an interior warmth.

In the spirituality of the Rosary, the past meets the present and is deeply intertwined with it. St. John Paul II explains that against "the background of the words *Ave Maria* the principal events of the life of Jesus Christ pass before the eyes of the soul. They take shape in the complete series of the joyful, sorrowful and glorious mysteries, and they put us in living communion with Jesus through—we might say—the heart of his Mother."[18] This communion that we have with Jesus through Mary resonates in how our own lives possess very real stages of joy, sorrow, light, and glory. At the same time, the pope emphasizes, we do not simply carry ourselves and our own lives to Jesus and Mary through the Rosary but we carry the lives of so many others as well: those whose presence we lovingly hold in our hearts as we offer our prayers. In the decades of the Rosary there are "all the events that make up the lives of individuals, families, nations, the Church, and all mankind. Our personal concerns and those of our neighbour,

---

[18] John Paul II, *Rosarium Virginis Mariae*, §2.

especially those who are closest to us, who are dearest to us. Thus the simple prayer of the Rosary marks the rhythm of human life."[19]

It does mark the rhythm of human life. Throughout centuries, this sacred and simple prayer has been used by heaven to help free souls from immorality, addiction, and sin; to win spiritual battles and even military battles that have affected the course of Western civilization; to help spiritually nourish souls; to bring peace to nations; and even to save human lives.[20]

✦ ✦ ✦ ✦ ✦ ✦ ✦

Shortly after Rosario was born, I received the honor of being asked to be the godfather of this beautiful baby girl. I was deeply moved by the request, knowing that this child is special: she was saved by heaven's intercession in a unique way and is beloved by the Almighty and by Mother Mary.

I think of the ripple effect that one life can have in this world. The character of Clarence the angel said it best to George Bailey (played, of course, by the inimitable Jimmy Stewart) in the classic film *It's a Wonderful Life*, after George was contemplating suicide and was shown by Clarence how many lives would have been affected for the worse were he never to exist.

"Strange, isn't it? Each man's life touches so many other lives," Clarence hauntingly tells George, later validating, "You see, George, you really had a wonderful life."[21]

In the case of Rosario, we had a real-life example of such a

---

[19] John Paul II, *Rosarium Virginis Mariae*, §2.

[20] To get a sense of the various historical victories that have been affected through the power of the Rosary, from victories against heresies to military battles that have impacted the survival and longevity of Christianity in Europe, I would—once again—recommend Fr. Donald Calloway's remarkable book *Champions of the Rosary: The History and Heroes of a Spiritual Weapon*.

[21] *It's a Wonderful Life*, directed by Frank Capra (Hollywood, CA: Paramount, 1946), https://www.youtube.com/watch?v=Lnqj06xMy_A.

possibility, of the potential of a person never existing (except in the womb). It is a reality that, unfortunately, has been the case for millions of unborn children who have never been given the chance of seeing the light of day through the sin of abortion, the sorrow of Our Lady's tears drenched with the blood of their innocent lives.

Rosario is a beautiful young girl today who laughs easily, encourages her father often, and brings the family great joy. She is also someone—her father has shared with me—who often has profound spiritual experiences of holy encounters. Yes, the graces of those thousands of prayers have worked deeply in her soul— and it is also a curious fact that it is sometimes children who, in their innocence, have the most sublime mystical encounters of the divine.

I love how the Rosary was such an instrumental prayer in saving her, such a spiritual weapon against the darkness that wanted to take this child's life; a perfect example of Our Lady crushing the serpent's head and protecting her children from his grasp, using the chain of the Rosary to subdue the evil one.

Lives will continue to be affected by her as Rosario keeps growing into a teenager and a young woman. How many can be touched for the better by a beautiful life. How different the world will be because she exists and is able to love and to pray, to teach, to honor God and neighbor with her presence, with her generosity, beauty, and intercession. I have little doubt that the Lord and Mother Mary will continue to guide her and have great plans for her, a child saved by grace. And I believe that Rosario was saved for a reason: to be a living miracle in this wounded world that is in desperate need of God's witnesses; to be a living testimony, a rose of wondrous beauty.

❧ Chapter 3 ❧

PRACTICING THE PRESENCE OF MARY

Do not fear to take Mary as your mother on the journey of life! May Mary be a model for you of how to follow Jesus. Do not be afraid of confiding in her, of entrusting to her maternal hands every problem, every anxiety, every expectation, and every project. Above all, trust her with the project that concerns your whole life: your vocation, in the sincere gift of what you are, for your own self-fulfillment.

—Pope St. John Paul II

There are many people who pray the Rosary, and read and pray with books on Marian consecration, consecrating themselves to the Mother of God. And yet, despite these noble spiritual pursuits, many still feel afterward like something is missing. They still feel as if they are not any closer in their relationship to Our Lady, not as close as they would like to be. Something in the relationship still needs work.

This chapter is about that missing link.

In one sense, it is very simple, identifying the missing link. Identifying it also becomes an opportunity to proactively practice a deeper Marian spirituality. So, what is the missing link?

It is this: people learn how to pray the Rosary as an intercessory prayer, they learn how to meditate on the mysteries of the Rosary, and they learn to consecrate themselves to Our Lady, allowing her the right to use their merits for the greatest benefit for the most souls. However, what they do not learn is the simple act of speaking to Our Lady from the heart.

Talk to her!

How can you have an intimate relationship with someone if you are unwilling to speak to that person and share with them your feelings and emotions, the depths of your heart?

I know a young woman who, when she was a little girl, would often draw with colored chalk on the sidewalk images of Our Lady, and while drawing she would speak to Mother Mary, speaking from the heart, a child to her mother, explaining how much she loves her, sharing about her day, cultivating a living relationship through simple, open conversation. Sometimes it is that simplicity of a child that can teach us greater depths of spirituality and Marian devotion than the most erudite and prolific Ivy League faculty of theology.

We need to ultimately learn how to speak to our Spiritual Mother and how to walk with her on a daily basis, treating her as a close, intimate friend—inviting her into a personal, intimate friendship. The most effective way that I have seen this spirituality articulated is from the work of the great twentieth-century Mariologist Fr. Emile Neubert, a theologian whose works were even read and loved by St. Maximilian Kolbe.

When you read Fr. Neubert's books on Marian spirituality and devotion, one fact quickly stands out—actually, it radiates from the pages—the fact that this man is absolutely in love with Our Lady. You can often tell by the words of an author whether they actually have an experiential, living relationship with the one they write about, or whether it is simply an academic exercise for them. When a person is in love, that love permeates their being, they cannot keep it to themselves and cannot hide it—and, in the case of a gifted writer and theologian, that love graciously radiates from the pages of the written text, pages that are touched by a spirit of prayer.

Fr. Neubert wrote a number of beautiful books about Our

Lady, among them *Life of Union with Mary*, one of the most powerful and moving books on Marian spirituality ever written. It is in *Life of Union with Mary* that Fr. Neubert articulates a spirituality known as practicing the "presence of Mary." Fr. Neubert explains that people have different personalities and cognitive inclinations, explaining that there are certain souls who are more visual and others who are less visual and more discursive. This affects how one practices the presence of Mary, as it is a meditative technique, and (as we have mentioned previously) meditation can be either visual or discursive. A person with a vivid imagination will be inclined toward the visual whereas a person with little or less of a visual imagination will be inclined toward the discursive, toward language.

Fr. Neubert quotes a person with "a rather vivid imagination," describing their practice of the presence of Mary:

> For some time I have experienced great joy in living in the presence of Mary. Whether I pray, play, or work, I see her image before me almost all the time. She is all beautiful, all pure. She looks at me, she smiles. I speak to her and feel immensely happy. Do not all persons who live in the presence of Mary see her, as I do, very close to them looking at them?[1]

Notice an important element of this spirituality: it is not restricted to "times of prayer," so to speak, or locations that we often associate as "places of prayer," such as a church, chapel, or a silent room. This spirituality is practiced throughout times, places, and situations—as the devotee explained, "Whether I pray, play, or work, I see her image before me almost all the time."

This is such a beautiful reality: to be so intimately in love with

---

[1] Fr. Emile Neubert, *Life of Union with Mary* (New Bedford, MA: Academy of the Immaculate, 2014), 54.

Our Lady that a person trains their mind and heart to constantly think of and "see" Mother Mary. That perpetual "seeing" makes it a spirituality of ceaseless prayer. Whether one is having coffee, taking a walk, sitting on the bench, cleaning their home, or preparing a meal, they can internally speak to Our Lady, orient their gaze, whether verbal or contemplative, toward her: thinking of her, loving her, allowing the affections of the heart to rise up to her as one takes a sip of their coffee, thinking of their beloved mom as being in front of them and with them.

Part of the power of a "presence of Mary" spirituality is that constantly speaking to her from the heart, invoking her name, contemplatively orienting one's loving gaze toward her throughout the day, becomes an invitation for her presence, for her motherly closeness and caress, to truly arrive and accompany a soul.

Often when I am hearing confessions, I feel inspired to cultivate in the penitents the practice of a presence of Mary spirituality by offering it as a penance. My framework is simple: they bring me, as the priest acting in the person of Christ, their sins, and after (through the power of Christ) I grant them absolution, cleansing them of their sins, I send them to Mother Mary for her maternal touch to continue to comfort, heal, and take care of them. I frequently tell a penitent, for their penance, to "take a walk with Mother Mary" as they leave the confessional and head to their next location, or to spend some time taking a walk with Mother Mary later that day. And to speak to her. To speak to her from the heart while visualizing her presence beside them. To share with her their struggles and ask for her loving intercession and guidance, or to share with her a personal expression of gratitude and love, as they are walking with her: gratitude and love for the sufferings that she endured for them at the foot of the Cross and for being a Spiritual Mother in their lives who constantly prays for them, intercedes for them, and loves them.

Similarly, in preaching, especially when I have the chance to preach retreats, taking the inspiration of Fr. Neubert's work,

I often encourage retreatants to begin to practice the presence of Mary in their daily lives. To come to the daily habit of visualizing her presence by their side, and to be vulnerable with her: to offer her their joys, struggles, fears, desires, even the smallest things that happen throughout the day. Most importantly, in encouraging this practice, what I hope to inspire in souls is a deep desire and daily habit of speaking to Our Lady from the heart, of getting used to regularly communicating with her like a child who is addressing his loving mother or intimate friend. My hope is that they come to understand that Mother Mary desires their intimacy, and that true intimacy comes from spending time with a person and vulnerably sharing with them—as she does with us when, through the mysteries of the Rosary, she shares her most intimate memories.

Not all people are very visual or imaginative; therefore, it becomes difficult for some to visualize Our Lady's presence beside them or even find constant inspiration from her images. Such individuals, possessing a more discursive mind, often need to turn toward words and language in their approach to Marian devotion. Fr. Neubert shares the testimony of a "person of little imagination," who writes that he placed a picture of the Virgin Mary on his desk to help him renew his devotion to her when glancing at the image, admitting that this worked only for a short while before it lost its efficacy.[2] "Then I would replace this picture with another, but after a time this one, too, lost its power of recall. After all, these pictures, even the most artistic of them, were so poor in comparison with the beauty which must have adorned the real Virgin."[3]

Having a discursive disposition, this devotee turned inward toward speech instead of relying on an image. It was still a "prayer of the heart"; he was concentrating on the presence of Mary but

---

[2] Neubert, *Life of Union with Mary*, 54.
[3] Neubert, *Life of Union with Mary*, 55.

with an interior movement of the mind and soul of simply speaking to her and gazing with affectionate love. "At present, I think periodically of Mary by pronouncing her name. I am like a child who under the eyes of its mother accomplished the work she has asked of me. Often the child raises its eyes toward her to testify to the joy there is in being able to serve her; then it continues to work under the spell of that joy and of the presence of its mother."[4] He continued to emphasize how this interior type of prayer of practicing the presence of Mary possesses the benefit of not having to obstruct work. "To look at Mary I do not have to detach my eyes from my work; by an interior glance that says 'Mary,' I encounter the loving glance of my mother. Instead of halting my work, this helps me to accomplish it with the greatest perfection possible because I put my whole soul into it."[5]

Here, there is a lived communion. This Marian soul, who in the inner depths of his heart and mind, regularly speaks to Mother Mary and, in a contemplative manner, "glances" at her, is able through an interior spiritual nourishment (that is provided by this communion) to be more alive and present to the tasks before him. This provides a perfect example of how a strong spirituality does not take a person away from the responsibilities of the world—in other words, spirituality is not a type of escapism—but actually helps a person become more robustly present and competent to rise up to the demands of life in the world.

Notice, additionally, how important it was for this Marian soul, again a more discursive soul, to invoke the sacred name of Mary. This is also an interior practicing of the presence of Mary that was instrumental in the life of the great French saint Louis de Montfort, who in his writings has given us some of the great treasures of Marian spirituality. A friend of de Montfort's reported: "The 'name of Mary' was constantly on his lips. . . . He took care to

---

4 Neubert, *Life of Union with Mary*, 55.
5 Neubert, *Life of Union with Mary*, 55.

make continual homage to her and the memory of the Mother of God was so imprinted on his mind and in his heart that he would never lose sight of it, so that, as he himself said to someone, he was constantly in the presence and under her eyes."[6]

What is important to realize is that there is real power in invoking a sacred name. For example, the most prominent form of ceaseless prayer in the Eastern Christian tradition, both Byzantine Catholic and Orthodox Christian, is to pray the Jesus Prayer: "Lord Jesus Christ, Son of God, have mercy on me, a sinner." One can pray the full prayer, or shorter expressions, such as "Lord Jesus, have mercy on me," or "Jesus, have mercy." The Jesus Prayer is especially popular in the monastic tradition of Eastern Christianity, many monks desiring to enter a state of ceaseless prayer by repeating the sacred words throughout the day; whether they are working, walking, or (some would even say) sleeping, the prayer becomes a part of them. It is not that they are simply praying but that they have become prayer. The prayer, being repeated countless times in the mind, can eventually make its way into the heart. This is a great grace when it happens, a grace from God that allows a person to experience the prayer in a deeper form, having moved from discursive meditation and into infused contemplation.[7]

Historian Steven Fanning writes of the Russian Orthodox mystic and staretz Silouan the Athonite (1866–1938), who entered the Russian monastery of St. Panteleimon on Mount

---

[6] As quoted in René Laurentin, *Mary in Scripture, Liturgy, and the Catholic Tradition*, trans. Sean O'Neill (Mahwah, NJ: Paulist Press, 2014), 114–15.

[7] A classic work of Russian spirituality that has popularized the Jesus Prayer and presents a hesychast spirituality of attaining ceaseless prayer and interior peace is the anonymous text *The Way of the Pilgrim*. For this work, combined with its sequel, see *The Way of the Pilgrim and The Pilgrim Continues His Way*, trans. Helen Bacovcin (New York: Image Books, 2003). The authoritative text on this spirituality is the *Philokalia*, a compilation of selected writings by the Eastern Fathers on the art of ceaseless prayer, virtue, and spirituality. See *Writings from the Philokalia on the Prayer of the Heart*, trans. E. Kadloubovsky and G. E. H. Palmer (UK: Faber and Faber, 1992).

Athos in 1892. After entering the novitiate, he was instructed in the Jesus Prayer and hesychastic spirituality, the art of ceaseless prayer and the grace of interior stillness. After only a few weeks of practicing this ceaseless prayer, he received the grace of infused contemplation, which he later attributed to the intercession of the Virgin Mary. "After only three weeks' practice of the Jesus Prayer, while standing before an ikon of the Virgin Mary, 'the prayer entered into his heart, to continue there, day and night, of its own accord.' At the time the simple young novice did not realize what a 'sublime and rare gift he had received from the Mother of God.'"[8]

What happens here pertains to the presence of God. When God's name is spoken in the Bible, there is also a self-revelation of God; that is, to speak His name is to invoke and invite His sacred presence. Thus, when a Christian is affectionately praying the Jesus Prayer, continually speaking the sacred name of Jesus in the inner depths of the mind and heart, the breathing rhythms of the devotee even come to correspond with the name of Jesus; as they inhale and breathe in the name of Jesus, they are also inviting His presence. Eventually, if the Lord allows a special grace, He can manifest His presence in a deeper way through what is known as infused contemplation.

Infused contemplation is a special grace of God—one that can only come from His side, not from ours—wherein one begins to experience a mystically supernatural stirring in the soul, feeling the presence of Another. That is, the Holy Spirit takes over the prayer—He becomes the primary mover of the prayer—and the Spirit begins, in a supernatural way, to pray in and through the person. The person begins to feel a supernatural presence within them, as the prayer transitions from the words of the Jesus Prayer spoken in the mind into a wordless, extraordinary grace

---

[8] Steven Fanning, *Mystics of the Christian Tradition* (London & New York: Routledge, 2001), 73. For an excellent biography of Silouan, see Archimandrite Sophrony, *The Monk of Mount Athos: Staretz Silouan 1866–1938*, trans. Rosemary Edmonds (Crestwood, NY: St. Vladimir's Seminary Press, 1989).

wherein the presence of God begins to inflame the heart and "speak" to it wordlessly through the consolations of a felt contemplative, spiritual union.

Through the affectionate repetition of the Jesus Prayer, a devotee has invited Jesus into a deeper interior intimacy, and the Lord can respond, if He chooses, by entering with infused contemplation. The mind becomes stiller as the soul experiences the supernatural presence of God like never before, in a direct, experiential infusion. Thus, the invocation of the name of Jesus actually invites the presence of Jesus in a more intimate expression of indwelling in the soul.

Similarly, behind the name of Jesus, the name of Mary is most sacred. Invoking her name, repeating it and praying it continually with loving affection, invites her spiritual presence more intimately into a person's life. Her mediation in a person's life becomes greater, as our Mother honors our free will and is immensely happy when we choose to invite her to a closer relationship.

When we consider the sacred power of Mary's name, there is an interesting correspondence toward how evil reacts to it. As we will see in a later chapter, demons fear her name and are repulsed by it with such intensity that they refuse to speak it during exorcisms. When Mother Mary appears during an exorcism, the sublime abundance of light that she carries brings spiritual pain to the demons, as it is painful for something dark to be in the presence of so much light. The invocation of her name, inviting her presence, brings dread to evil, whereas it brings joy and healing to the faithful.

The Presence of Mary as a Spiritual Gift

For a number of saints, from ages past to contemporary figures, the practice of the presence of Mary was essential to cultivating their daily spiritual lives, their union with the Mother of God, and their path of sanctification with Christ. Whether it was St. Louis de Montfort, or St. John Paul II, who often spoke to Our Lady and "felt" her presence, those who have experienced this Marian spirituality "see it as one of the keys to holiness, zeal, faithfulness, effectiveness, and joy that can overcome any cross."[9]

Fr. René Laurentin, a French priest who was one of the most prolific and eminent Mariologists of the twentieth century, takes the concept of the "presence of Mary" deeper by acknowledging that it is not just a practice but also a spiritual gift, a special grace given by God. In other words, it "is a gift and not a commodity that is acquired through our effort alone; like all spiritual gifts, it may be desired and asked for. We can make ourselves ready to receive it and have it grow freely. The gift and the effort (our responsiveness) normally both require each other."[10]

What exactly does he mean here? After all, did we not just discuss how practicing a presence of Mary spirituality requires a meditative effort, whether visual or discursive, on our end?

What Fr. Laurentin is getting at is the distinction between practicing meditation and experiencing infused contemplation within the context of a presence of Mary spirituality. We begin with meditation, using our imagination or our interior dialogue to speak to Mother Mary from the depths of our hearts. This is a fruitful, proactive spirituality wherein we make a deliberate effort to engage our Spiritual Mother. Certainly there may be a grace that's present pulling us toward her, or affecting our disposition, and the meditation can become a response to that actual grace.

However, it does not have to end there. Some souls, practicing a presence of Mary spirituality, have been taken beyond meditative prayer and into the mystical prayer of infused contemplation, wherein the presence of Mary is experienced through an extraordinary grace in a supernaturally higher way.

There was a moment in my life when I was blessed to receive

---

[9] Laurentin, *Mary in Scripture*, 163.
[10] Laurentin, *Mary in Scripture*, 162.

this grace, by no merit of my own as it was pure gift. A beautiful soul, a woman with a very deep mystical life and charismatic gifts, who is a spiritual directee and a dear friend of mine, prayed with me, and in the midst of the prayer I experienced the grace of the presence of Mary in a supernaturally tangible way that lasted for days, perhaps about two weeks or so, thereafter. In that time, I felt the presence of Mother Mary like never before: my heart burning with a fervor and love for her, my mind thinking of her constantly, my soul experiencing a deep freedom and peace, even in the midst of a yearning that, at times, hurt because it desired her presence so intensely, the interior aches of longing for a beloved.

But that freedom and peace are real because it is the freedom of knowing that you are loved intensely and *feeling* the overwhelming intensity of that love. When that mystical love envelops your inner life, nothing else matters, and nothing really bothers you. No rude word, no abrasive personality or difficult situation—none of it "gets through," none of it interrupts your inner tranquility, because your consolation, peace, strength, and meaning are found in the love that is penetrating and inflaming the innermost part of your soul. She is there, that beautiful woman for whom you are willing to give everything and for whom you are willing to endure anything. In the intimacy of the relationship, you have found your freedom.

For the sake of proper theology, we must be careful, however, with the words "she is there" when speaking about the presence of Mary within the soul. What happens when a person experiences a special, contemplative grace of the presence of Mary, to the point that they feel her love not only beside them but also within them, is actually a movement of the Holy Spirit in the soul, who is truly present within. That is to say, it is the Spirit who is actually experienced *within*. However, it is an interior movement of the Holy Spirit that is very specifically mediated by Our Lady, who is the spouse of the Spirit, and thus her presence is felt in that mediation. One feels the sweet caress of her touch as she is mediating the presence of the Spirit, who is the source of the grace. Thus, she does not actually reside within but she does affect the grace that is felt within.[11]

Fr. Neubert elaborates, "If, as we shall see, a certain number of Marian souls speak of the presence of Mary within them, we must understand the word 'presence' as an almost constant awareness of the action of Mary in their interior."[12] Notice the essential theological distinction here: a person can have an "almost constant awareness" of the action of Mary affecting their soul, but that does not mean that she is actually residing within the person's soul. She is affecting a person's interior life, acting upon it with her loving and maternal influence, but it is the Holy Spirit who is the presence acting within; yet that spiritual activity within the soul still has a strong Marian dimension of her gently (or, at times, intensely) felt maternal mediation.

St. Maximilian Kolbe had a very robust Mariology, which he connected to pneumatology, the technical expression for the "study of the Holy Spirit." In Kolbe's theology, Mary and the Holy Spirit are so deeply united that the Holy Spirit never acts without her.[13] Other theologians may argue this point, but what is unarguable is that when a person is experiencing a special grace of the presence of Mary, that is exactly what is happening. The Holy Spirit is acting within the soul, providing the tangible sweetness of the experience, but it is experienced through her mediation and

---

[11] See Laurentin, *Mary in Scripture*, 127. Fr. Neubert is clear to make the distinction that "Mary does not [actually] reside in the soul," and he quotes Fr. William Joseph Chaminade, the French founder of the Marianists, as explaining, when speaking of the spiritual gift of the presence of Mary, that "the Blessed Virgin is not in our midst in the same way as our Lord Jesus Christ." Neubert, *Life of Union with Mary*, 220.

[12] Neubert, *Life of Union with Mary*, 220.

[13] For a great synthesis of Maximilian Kolbe's Mariology and its rich relationship to pneumatology, see Fr. H. M. Manteau-Bonamy, O.P., *Immaculate Conception and the Holy Spirit: The Marian Teachings of St. Maximilian Kolbe* (Libertyville, IL: Franciscan Marytown Press, 1977).

presence, her special relationship and intercession in the person's life. Thus, it is an intimacy that is sweetly Marian, leading to a great experience and love of God in the soul.

Affective Union with Her

Elaborating on the work of the great Dominican theologian Fr. Réginald Garrigou-Lagrange, Fr. Laurentin articulates a distinction between two ways to love, through a real union and through an affective union. "Real union" pertains to two people being physically present to each other, thus being in each other's company, whereas "affective union" pertains to the love that is inspired in the mind and soul through the felt absence of the beloved. The very nature of spiritual love on earth, as it means a love for Jesus and Mary who in their bodies are in heaven, has the quality of affective union.[14] That affective union can be seen in two ways: *amantum est in amante*, meaning "the beloved person is in the one who loves, through the kindness that she inspires in him," or *amans est in amato*, meaning "the person who loves is within the beloved, as he very powerfully and intimately welcomes what makes that person happy."[15]

This constitutes another meaningful expression of living out the presence of Mary.

Thus, even though there is a "distance" because I cannot see her face-to-face, because we are not physically present to each other, in the yearning and affectionate "memory" that the distance provides there is presence, her presence, because the thought of her inspires a warming intimacy in my heart for her. And, through

---

[14] Laurentin, *Mary in Scripture*, 130. For Garrigou-Lagrange's great work in systematic Mariology, which Laurentin is making reference to, see Réginald Garrigou-Lagrange, OP, *Mother of the Saviour and Our Interior Life*, trans. Fr. Bernard J. Kelly, CSSp (Charlotte, NC: TAN Books, 2012). Garrigou-Lagrange's Mariological magnum opus was first published in 1948.

[15] Laurentin, *Mary in Scripture*, 130.

that sacred thought and the fire of love that she moves in my heart, she makes me a better person, more virtuous and loving to others as I desire to live for her and to make her happy. To bring her joy is one of my deepest desires. And I know that what brings her joy is the nourishment of my soul, the growth in purity and charity that is cultivated *within* by how it transforms me and *without* by how it affects others.

The thought of her makes me want to be a better person; it inspires kindness and generosity in my soul, for that is what she would want from me and for me. And here is the paradox: though she is not physically present, I carry her in my heart. Thus, while there is physical distance between us, it inspires an emotional longing that affects me spiritually. The yearning for her, especially the deep desire to see her one day, makes me want to live a life of virtue and spiritual growth, as that becomes the door that will one day lead me to truly encounter her face-to-face, that will remove all distance and take our relationship from affective union to real union. That moment, for which I am living and which love is driving me towards, orients and shapes my daily decisions. It should affect every decision that I make during the day. She, therefore, becomes my *Why*, the person for whom I am living and whom I am honoring through my daily moral choices, spiritual practices, and sacrifices.

For the Love of Mary: The Witness of Maximilian Kolbe

Living in the presence of Mary—a person who understood this way of life well, who lived for her almost every day since his youth, in good times and in bad, in sickness and in health, is the great Polish Franciscan priest, martyr, and saint Maximilian Maria Kolbe. Writing of Kolbe, the French writer and biographer André Frossard highlighted how Kolbe received great spiritual and moral energy in contemplating the sublime mystery of Mary, of who she was, of her Immaculate Conception, of her person. This contemplation of her, Kolbe's biographer explains, "fortified him; it ordered his thought; it liberated him. And his view of the world was gently noble, the view of those whom nothing troubles, nothing frightens, who know where they have come from and where they are going. At Auschwitz, he lived only for her."[16]

The final part of Frossard's observation is striking. Kolbe was a prisoner in Auschwitz who was cruelly subjected to horrible abuse and humiliation as a Catholic priest, yet somehow he was able to become a living light in that hellish prison of human sorrow and suffering. A radiant charity toward others illumined from his soul, culminating in the final act of selfless, iconic sacrifice whose heroic magnitude has spread far beyond the barriers of the concentration camp and has reached the ends of the earth. People today know the moment well—what happened when a prisoner escaped from the concentration camp and, as a reprisal, the SS decided to pick out and punish ten prisoners by sending them to a starvation bunker. Many decades later, people around the world know about it, and talk about it, and are inspired by it, as nothing of the sort has been witnessed before: a priest stepping out of line and voluntarily offering to sacrifice his life, through the slow and painful interior torture that is dying naked in a starvation bunker, for a stranger, one of the ten chosen, who in desperation pleaded to be saved so he could see his wife and children again.

It was one of the greatest imitations of the Passion of Jesus Christ, the innocent offering himself for the salvation of others in a cruel and horrible death, that has ever been witnessed in human history; the priest, in this case, becoming a living icon of Christ crucified, his death in Auschwitz, that modern Golgotha, inspiring a hope that would not only save the life of one man but also light a match that would affect countless generations to come by

---

[16] André Frossard, *Forget Not Love: The Passion of Maximilian Kolbe*, trans. Cendrine Fontan (San Francisco, CA: Ignatius Press, 1991), 57.

bearing witness to what it means to be an authentic disciple of Christ through the love of Mary.

I like to think that when Franciszek Gajowniczek, the Polish army sergeant whose life was saved by Kolbe, broke down in desperation when the SS officers chose him to be one of the prisoners to die, that the Spirit which inspired Maximilian Kolbe to take his place also took Kolbe back to his childhood, in an instantaneous moment of intuitive nostalgia, to the vision that changed his life. It was as a child that the young Raymond Kolbe (his name before assuming the religious name of Maximilian) experienced a vision of the Virgin Mary. The prayer of his heart was "What will become of me?" She appeared to him and presented an answer, offering the Polish child two crowns, a white one representing chastity and a red one representing martyrdom. "Which one do you want?" the Blessed Mother asked, honoring his free will.

The young Kolbe chose both crowns.

Perhaps in that moment in Auschwitz, so many years later, seconds before he did the unthinkable and stepped out of line to offer his life for a suffering soul, the image of the red crown came back to him, and the kind, maternal voice of his great love, the Immaculate Virgin Mary, could be felt in his spirit, taking him back to his childhood encounter and gently saying—even if not audibly—"My beloved, it's time . . . it's time."

I like to think that even Karl Fritzsch—the notorious SS deputy who, outraged by the fact that this prisoner dared to step out of line and approach him, and after asking Kolbe's profession was told "I am a Catholic priest"—had a place in the depths of his wounded, darkened heart that was strangely touched by the unthinkable gesture. After all, he could have not allowed it. He could have ordered Kolbe to get back in line, or could have killed him on the spot for stepping out, refusing to allow the heroic action of the Polish priest to permeate the camp grounds and to spread to the ears of the other prisoners in order to stifle any semblance of hope in their minds. But he did allow it. And he did allow Franciszek Gajowniczek to live. And the act of goodness did permeate the barracks of the camp, reminding the other prisoners that in the midst of all the horror, misery, and senseless suffering and shame that they had to endure, there were still traces of kindness and light left in the world. There were still those who showed by their sacrifices that God is real and has not forgotten the suffering. There were still saints among us.

Frossard, in his elegant biography of Kolbe, *Forget Not Love: The Passion of Maximilian Kolbe*, a work which I will rely on heavily to form the narrative of the next pages, describes an incident wherein the Franciscan priest was severely beaten:

> A Schaufuhrer, a sergeant, belonging doubtless to that hybrid species of Sicherheitsdienst, or "security service," a cross between the Gestapo and the SS, pounced on Kolbe one day, snatched the rosary he wore on his belt, and showing him the crucifix, demanded to know if he really believed in it. Kolbe having responded, "Yes," the Schaufuhrer struck him in the face. Then he repeated his question several times, and as he obtained the same response each time, he struck each time. When he left, Kolbe's comrades, seeing him praying, approached to comfort him. But he told them not to worry about him, that what had happened was nothing, that he withstood those things without pain for love of Mary. He continued his prayer, and, according to the witnesses, had not his face been red from the blows, one would have thought that nothing had happened.[17]

Notice how vividly and consistently Kolbe practiced a presence of Mary spirituality. Even in the midst of dehumanizing torment at the hands of evil, his very sacred devotion of the Rosary being

---

[17] Frossard, *Forget Not Love*, 178.

violently mocked as he was being beaten, emulating the way that the crown of thorns was blasphemously used to ridicule Christ's royal dignity, Kolbe was still thinking of the presence of Mary and offering every pain for love of her.

The presence of Mary in the life of St. Maximilian Kolbe led him, in those darkest hours, to a spirituality that was not just passive but active in its burning charity. This meant, for Kolbe, that practicing a presence of Mary spirituality did not mean simply offering up every pain and humiliation that he experienced to Mary as an act of love but also proactively seeking out the most oppressed, disheartened, and despairing souls around him in that prison of human suffering that is a concentration camp to offer care and consolation.

It is as if Our Lady were walking the camp grounds herself, using the hands of a soul consecrated and surrendered to her to bring her maternal care to her sorrowful children. Remember, when a person truly lives a presence of Mary spirituality, it becomes an invitation for her actual presence. Her light shines through that soul.

"One day he was beaten senseless and left for dead by the guards. He was taken to the hospital, running a fever, his face swollen. He said nothing. He was given the last free place, in the draft at the door. He appreciated this. It allowed him to welcome the sick with a kind word and to pray for the dead as they were carried out."[18]

Frossard pondered that it "was hard to know from where that sickly, abused creature drew his force, or where that sick man found the hope that he distributed all around him as if it were Communion."[19] Victor Frankl famously wrote that those souls were able to endure the concentration camps who had a greater *Why* that they were living for, a deeper purpose or meaning in

---

[18] Frossard, *Forget Not Love*, 190.
[19] Frossard, *Forget Not Love*, 190.

their lives that kept them going, nourishing the mental and spiritual stamina necessary for inner strength. For Kolbe, that *Why* was a person; it was the love of his life, Mary Immaculate. But Kolbe's Marian devotion was not just interior or private; it was apostolic and evangelistic. He saw the world like a missionary, any situation that he was placed in as an opportunity to spread the love of God through Mary. His actions in Auschwitz show that he lived out his imprisonment the same way, a missionary of hope ministering to a populace of sorrow.

There is a lesson here for us. A presence of Mary spirituality should lead to a moral and spiritual response in our lives. That is to say, it is a relationship, and any relationship, in order to flourish, requires work; that means our own loving response, which often can be challenging, especially when we do not feel consolations in our day—but that is how true love is proven; you do what you need to do for the beloved whether you feel like it or not. No matter how difficult our days or personal situations are, we need to remind ourselves of the example of our spiritual forefathers and foremothers who had to sacrifice so much and still loved radically.

When we simply consider the horrors of the twentieth century—the wars, the concentration camps, the murder of the innocent, the torture of human beings, the desecration of human dignity, the forced separation of families, Nazism, Communism, the systematic persecution of religious belief—and how much people had to endure, so many in the midst of these unbearable trials staying true to Jesus and His Church, exuding a strength and martyrdom that was both interior and at times exterior, we come to realize how much we have been given. We realize not to take it for granted; we come to realize how good we have it, in comparison, and how because people had to suffer so much, we owe it to them to live our best lives, to make daily sacrifices that will honor the moral and spiritual dignity of our souls and that of our brothers and sisters, that will honor the memory of those whose lives ended too soon and whose eyes had to see too much ugliness during the period they had to live in this world.

The psychologist Jordan Peterson has written beautifully about these realities. Peterson articulates how each of us has a responsibility for our daily tasks and moral obligations—even the smallest, from making a meal more delicious, cleaning one's room, attending to the stack of paperwork that has been piling up—and that we should perform these tasks with an awareness, both historical and spiritual, of the suffering of those who have come before and the gift of our existence that should never be taken for granted. He writes:

> You may find that if you attend to these moral obligations, once you have placed "make the world better" at the top of your value hierarchy, you experience ever-deepening meaning. It's not bliss. It's not happiness. It's something more like atonement for the criminal fact of your fractured and damaged Being. It's payment of the debt you owe for the insane and horrible miracle of your existence. It's how you remember the Holocaust. It's how you make amends for the pathology of history. It's adoption of the responsibility for being a potential denizen of Hell. It is willingness to serve as an angel of Paradise.[20]

At Auschwitz, Maximilian Kolbe served as an angel of Paradise.

When I consider how much that man had to endure—the misery of Auschwitz combined with the additional harassment of being a priest who was targeted for special cruelty—and realize that he never gave up his deep Marian devotion or faith in God but lived out a presence of Mary spirituality to the very end, it reminds me that I have no excuses in my daily life. Jesus made it

---

[20] Jordan B. Peterson, *12 Rules for Life: An Antidote to Chaos* (Toronto, Canada: Random House Canada, 2018), 200.

clear: "If any man would come after me, let him deny himself and take up his cross daily and follow me" (Luke 9:23).

Often in the confessional, I hear penitents explaining that they have been lazy in their spiritual lives, in daily prayer, in concentrating on Jesus and Mary, because they have felt dryness or a lack of consolation from God. What is troubling and discouraging about this pattern of thought is that it reduces the responsibilities of faith to feelings. If I feel the consolations, I will honor the relationship. If I do not, I'll turn to other things. There's no sacrifice, there's no acceptance of the Cross, just a life revolving around comfort and feelings. It is a mockery to those who have come before and have had to sacrifice so much, persevering in their faith through it all.

I don't believe that Kolbe felt many consolations at Auschwitz; neither did Jesus at Calvary when, from the depths of His soul, He yelled out, "My God, my God, why have you forsaken me?" (Matt 27:46). But a man of genuine faith is not a slave to his feelings. True love is not about being swayed by feelings but about the selfless determination of one's will, surrendering to grace; it is about choosing to do what is right, what honors the beloved, whether or not the feelings are in line. Kolbe's strong faith, his unspeakable love for the Virgin Mary, did not break in the midst of the surrounding darkness or the inner anguish that he, a sensitive soul witnessing so much human suffering, must have experienced; but it nourished an interior strength that allowed him to spiritually transcend his miserable circumstances.

The surrounding evil could not touch him. Physically, they could abuse him; emotionally, they could ridicule him; but spiritually, on that deepest level of the soul where the greatest consequences lie—the eternal destination of the human being, the arena of the great battle between Christ and the devil—they could not break him. In that sense, Prisoner 16670 was the freest of men.

"A prince among us," one witness at Auschwitz testified.[21]

Kolbe realized that he couldn't just turn in on himself in the midst of the horrible cruelty he was subjected to but must, out of love for the Mother of God, come out of himself and serve others. He saw the horror of Auschwitz as an opportunity for immense charity, seeing every humiliation as a sacrifice he could offer up. "All, Jews or Christians, priests or ministers, with death all around, saw Kolbe unconcerned about his own fate, too concerned with others to be worried about himself, and seeing everywhere those more unhappy and more pitiful than himself."[22]

At the great Marian apparitions of Fatima, which happened in 1917, the year that Lenin and the Bolsheviks had their revolution in Russia leading to the formation of the Soviet Union and the year that a young Maximilian Kolbe was inspired to found the Militia of the Immaculata, Our Lady said to the visionaries to make of everything they could a sacrifice to God, an offering for reparation. That is exactly how Kolbe lived out his imprisonment at Auschwitz. "He lived on what was refused him, he fortified himself with what should have crushed him, and when someone tried to humiliate him, he offered his honor for humanity."[23]

Such is the profound freedom of the saints. They care less about themselves and more about those around them. They care less about their comfort and more about whether they are pleasing God.

"What could they do to Kolbe? He lived his imprisonment like a special mission, his only concern that he might be unworthy of it," Frossard explains.[24]

It happened until the final moments of his life. After the ten prisoners were chosen to enter the starvation bunker, their fate in this world forever sealed—never would they have another moment

---

[21] As quoted in Frossard, *Forget Not Love*, 192.

[22] Frossard, *Forget Not Love*, 191.

[23] Frossard, *Forget Not Love*, 191.

[24] Frossard, *Forget Not Love*, 191.

on this earth to see their families, their friends, or loved ones again ("It's all over," the despairing mind could say)—and after Kolbe volunteered to be one of them, a witness observing the scene from a window noticed that as the men walked toward the barrack that would be their last destination on earth, being pushed by the SS, "Maximilian Kolbe walked last, supporting a comrade."[25]

Not one opportunity for charity, for helping another and consoling human sorrow, was wasted by this generous Marian soul.

Starvation and dehydration lead to a slow, excruciating, and painful death, physical agony combined with mental degradation. "Hunger is terrible; thirst is even worse. Dehydration attacks the brain cells first and unleashes silent storms of nightmares and hallucinations."[26] However, even in the starvation bunker, to the very last moments that he could, Kolbe's faith and Marian love brought hope. Subjected to dehumanizing conditions, the men were stripped naked and enclosed in a small cell together. Kolbe encouraged them, led them in Marian hymns, and prayed with them and over the dying. Those who passed by and heard them singing said it felt like being in church.

Eventually an order was given to finish off the survivors. Kolbe was one of the last men still breathing. It was the vigil of the Assumption, the great solemnity celebrating the passing of the Virgin Mary from this life into heaven. A syringe of carbolic acid was injected into the body of Maximilian Kolbe. Frossard poignantly compares the moment to the soldiers approaching Jesus's body and piercing it with a lance. "That is how Maximilian Kolbe died and with him the very pure child who had so loved the Virgin Mary."[27]

✦ ✦ ✦ ✦ ✦ ✦ ✦

---

[25] Frossard, *Forget Not Love*, 197.
[26] Frossard, *Forget Not Love*, 198.
[27] Frossard, *Forget Not Love*, 199.

It is often the case that when a person of deep holiness who has led an incredibly meaningful life given over to God dies, their death transpires on a date that is providential. Thus, when Pope St. John Paul II, posthumously and appropriately known as "John Paul the Great," died, it was on the eve of Divine Mercy Sunday, the great feast day that he instituted in honor of the request that Jesus made in His revelations to the Polish mystic and saint Sister Faustina Kowalska. Through the great feast day and supporting its devotion, John Paul II helped bring to the Church and to the world a deeper understanding of God's divine mercy and a massive outpouring of graces, especially through a renewal of the sacrament of confession.

When Fr. Benedict Groeschel, one of the main founders of the Franciscan Friars of the Renewal and a spiritual giant in twentieth-century Catholicism, died, it was on the vigil of the feast day of St. Francis of Assisi. Before the feast day itself, which is October 4, Franciscans around the world celebrate the "transitus" of St. Francis, the eve on which Francis passed from this life and into eternity. How appropriate that the spiritual figurehead behind a movement that would renew the Franciscan charism of poverty and prayer in the twentieth century passed away on this day.

And, of course, how appropriate and fitting that St. Maximilian Maria Kolbe, that great apostle of the Blessed Virgin Mary, who had given his entire life over to her since that sacred moment of encounter as a child, passed away on the vigil of the Assumption, the day that we celebrate her passing from this life and into eternity.

I have known people who have been present at the deathbeds of their relatives or loved ones, relatives who have led devout lives, and who moments before their deaths—literally seconds before their final breath—have pointed to a space in the room or have acknowledged that she is there, that they see the Blessed Virgin Mary. Then they take their final breath.

What exactly is happening in those final moments?

The skeptic may argue that it is wishful thinking, or a pious hallucination as health is declining and the brain is in its final stages of operation, but the truth is that, in the face of death, skepticism has no real answers. What I believe is happening in those moments, as it is not a rare occurrence among devout people, is an answer to prayer. For some, it is an answer to their daily prayers, particularly the second half of the Hail Mary, when throughout their lives devotees have lovingly offered the request to the Holy Mother, "Pray for us sinners, now and at the hour of our death."

How can the most loving mother, as she is, not reply to the sincerity of that plea from a loyal child? St. Maximilian Kolbe once proclaimed, "Oh, Immaculate! How sweet will be the death of those who belong to you!"[28]

But, of course, she is also Mother of Mercy, and in that hour of death, I have little doubt, there have been great sinners who (through the inspiration of grace) have called out to her for assistance and protection. Even the great Italian poet Dante Alighieri depicted such a scene in the *Purgatorio*:

> There I went blind. I could no longer speak,
>> but as I died, I murmured Mary's name,
>> and there I fell and left my empty flesh.
> Now hear the truth. Tell it to living men:
>> God's angel took me up, and Hell's fiend cried:
>> "O you from Heaven, why steal what is mine?"[29]

The voice that speaks in the canto is that of Buonconte I da Montefeltro, who was an Italian Ghibelline general. Katarzyna Dudek, professor of English literature and my colleague in

---

28 HM Television, "Saint Maximilian Mary Kolbe," YouTube video, 30:27, August 11, 2014, https://www.youtube.com/watch?v=THT5QxhCiGE.

29 Dante Alighieri, *Purgatorio*, canto 5, lines 88–108, in *The Portable Dante*, trans. and ed. Mark Musa (New York: Penguin Books, 2003), 221.

Austria, explains that Buonconte "suffered death on a battlefield and his body was never found. Dante came up with an idea that Buonconte experienced a last-minute conversion and his soul was taken up by an angel, yet the body was mutilated by the devil who was enraged by losing his prey."[30]

Notice how it was simply speaking the sacred name of Mary, calling out to her at the moment of death from the interior depths of his agonizing soul, in an occasion of pure repentance, that led Buonconte to receive the graces of salvation, according to Dante's depiction. There is a theme here. She is a powerful intercessor at the moment of death. The early and medieval Christians knew this well, and many modern people have also experienced this sublime reality very personally.[31]

There is a remarkable freedom that Marian souls possess, those who in this life have decided to live for her and in her presence. When this life ends, they welcome death because they anticipate to truly be in her presence. It is the day they have been waiting for, for many years. And with it, the fear of death is no more.

---

[30] Personal correspondence with the author. My gratitude to Dr. Dudek for initially informing me of this passage from Dante and for the corresponding commentary.

[31] The oldest Marian prayer that we have is known as the *Sub Tuum Praesidium*, dated as early as AD 250. The text of the short prayer invokes Our Lady as Mother of God and asks for her protection and intercession: "We fly to thy patronage, O holy Mother of God; despise not our petitions in our necessities, but deliver us always from all dangers, O glorious and blessed Virgin. Amen." The historical relevance of the prayer is that it was invoked by the early Christian communities in the midst of periods of persecution, signifying that in the face of death, early Christians implored the protection of their heavenly Mother.

Chapter 4

WHY DOES OUR MOTHER WEEP?

Devotion to the Mother of Sorrows

Simeon's words ["A sword shall pierce your heart"] seem like a second Annunciation to Mary, for they tell her of the actual historical situation in which the Son is to accomplish his mission, namely, in misunderstanding and sorrow.

—*Pope St. John Paul II*

In an instant, I saw horrible things: the executioners left Jesus, and other people started scourging Him; they seized the scourges and struck the Lord mercilessly. These were priests, religious men and women; and high dignitaries of the Church, which surprised me greatly. There were lay people of all ages and walks of life. All vented their malice on the innocent Jesus. Seeing this, my heart fell as if into a mortal agony.

—*St. Faustina Kowalska, Diary entry 445.*

When I was a child in Chicago, I remember one late afternoon watching television with my family in our living room; most likely (if my memory serves me correctly) we were watching a Chicago Bulls game. It was the 1990s, and to my young mind—as for many Chicagoans back then—Michael Jordan and the Bulls were the center of the world, our joy and our devotion, at times our obsession. There was a commercial break, and a number of news stories came up, briefly highlighting stories that would be featured on the news after the game. There was one story that, when it came up and I saw those hauntingly powerful images, stunned me to the most inner core of my being. My young heart and soul felt pierced when I saw it, and for the shortest of moments, Michael Jordan did not exist anymore. My obsession and devotion would turn elsewhere.

The news story showed footage of a statue of the Virgin Mary in a Catholic parish that started weeping tears of blood; the phenomenon was caught on tape, and we saw the blood-stained tears dripping from the eyes and down the face of Our Lady to the lower parts of the statue.

I was haunted by that image.

As a child, there were at least two elements about the footage of the weeping Virgin that stunned me with such unexpected awe. First, I had no idea that such events, supernatural phenomena, happen. I went to public schools where we did not study religion, and during our Saturday CCD classes at the parish no one taught us about such happenings—and we *never* heard of them being preached about at Mass. Second, if this was an authentic supernatural occurrence—which I believed it was—then why, I wondered as a child, was Our Lady crying? Why was she weeping in such a vivid, and somewhat grotesque, way, tears of blood falling from her eyes? Why does our Mother weep?

To this day, I do not know which parish it was, or whether the diocese ever officially investigated or ruled on the phenomenon. To this day, I don't have to know. Because what I do know today is that the supernatural and the miraculous are real. We have a faith that is predicated upon the supernatural and miraculous: without the Incarnation, the Resurrection, the healing miracles of Jesus—all supernatural occurrences—our faith means nothing. Throughout history, even after His Resurrection and Ascension, the Lord has continued to work in His supernatural power with various events—miraculous healings, Marian apparitions, Eucharistic miracles, exorcisms, stigmata wounds, bleeding statues—to give us signs that lead us back to conversion and Gospel living.

To show us that God *is*, and not *was*; to show us that His supernatural power and presence are real.

Little did I know back then, as the images of the weeping Virgin statue consumed my mind and the seeds of something holy and pure were stirred and awakened within my soul, that much of my life as an adult would be dedicated to these two expressions of faith: the Marian and the supernatural. I would go on to study Christian spirituality in graduate school, writing my doctoral dissertation on Marian apparitions, mysticism, and mystical theology, topics that I would eventually teach about in Mariology classes to college students.

At times, throughout the years, that question would come back to me: Why does our Mother weep? Little did I know, as a child, that there is a rich history of devotion in Christian spirituality dedicated to Our Lady's sorrows. To truly have a relationship with Our Lady, a person needs to delve into the depths of her sorrows and realize that in that place of suffering, a person can also bring their own sufferings to her, intimately meeting her at the foot of the Cross, where our wounds are united to her wounds as together we contemplate the face of her crucified Son. It is there, at the foot of the Cross, that the truest intimacy and the meaning of life are found.

Devotion to the Mother of Sorrows

I currently live and minister in Gaming, Austria, a small town where Franciscan University of Steubenville has its study abroad program, situated at the Kartause, a medieval Carthusian monastery located at the foothills of the Alps whose halls today function as classrooms, dormitories, and a refectory for our predominantly Catholic students. One of the privileges and joys of this ministry is the opportunity to travel on pilgrimage with our students to the sacred sites of Europe, including many of the great Marian shrines. When a person is able to encounter the great churches, basilicas, and cathedrals of Austria, Poland, Italy, and Germany, especially from the perspective of American eyes, one thing becomes clear: there is a world of difference between the art and architecture of the Old World and the New World, between Europe and the United States. That world of difference also speaks to a history of devotion that was prominent in the culture.

So many of the European churches, both East and West, both small parishes and massive basilicas, are expressions of the Gothic and baroque styles of art and architecture; certain churches—like a number of the churches in Kraków, resembling the grandeur of Polish church architecture—are a combination of the Gothic and baroque. Within such churches you will often see a devotional depiction that is rare in American churches: a sculpture or painting of Our Lady as *Mater Dolorosa*, Mother of Sorrows. It is usually a vivid depiction of Mary that shows an anguished and sorrowful expression on her face and that includes a sword piercing her heart, or frequently seven swords piercing her heart, the latter being a representation of the Seven Sorrows of Mary devotion. The Seven Sorrows of Mary devotion flourished in late-medieval Christian spirituality, which emphasized the sufferings of Mother Mary at the foot of the Cross and in relation to the life of her Son, Jesus: the Mother intimately sharing, like no one else, in the sorrows of her Son.

There were numerous factors—historical, spiritual, and cultural—in late-medieval Europe that played a role in inspiring and increasing devotion to the sorrowful Mother. Among them was the period of the Crusades, military operations to the Middle East wherein many young men were sent to fight and whose lives were lost. Families experienced the pain of what it means to have a son killed, a pain that Our Lady in her sorrow understood too well. The years 1347–1351 also saw the most fatal pandemic in history, the Black Death, spread throughout Europe and Northern Africa, killing an estimated 75–200 million people. In other words, disease, mortality, and untimely death of loved ones surrounded the culture. Turning to faith and spirituality, grieving souls were able to unite their sorrows spiritually with Our Lady's grief, knowing that she especially can understand their struggles and perhaps even offer some consolation, even the consolation of *suffering together*, in the midst of all the pain.

Pilgrims were also making the journey to Jerusalem, encountering the *Via Dolorosa*, the way of sorrow that Jesus walked toward Calvary. Eventually, the spirituality was brought back to Europe through the Stations of the Cross. The idea was that through the Stations a person can make a "mini-pilgrimage" along Jesus's way of sorrow, especially if one does not have the means to travel to the Holy Land. The Franciscans were particularly devoted to bringing this spirituality of the Passion back to Europe. In the fifteenth and sixteenth centuries the friars were involved in the construction of a number of outdoor shrines that incorporated the Stations and were replicas of sacred sites that they encountered in the Holy Land.

Spiritually, the Cistercian and Franciscan orders played a major influence in spreading the devotion to both the Passion and Our Lady as Mother of Sorrows. The homilies, spiritual writings, and prayers of great Cistercian monks like St. Bernard of Clairvaux and Amadeus of Lausanne, abbot and bishop, gave emphasis to the Passion, and in that Passion spirituality to the sufferings that Mother Mary endured as a co-sufferer with Jesus.[1] The Franciscans would follow in advancing this spirituality even further.[2]

---

[1]   See Eva De Visscher, "Marian Devotion in the Latin West in the Later Middle Ages," in *Mary: The Complete Resource*, ed. Sarah Jane Boss (New York: Oxford University Press, 2007), 182–83.

[2]   Thomas Bestul explains that in "the thirteenth century, Franciscan spirituality carried devotion to the suffering humanity of Christ to new heights. The chief literary products of this devotion were written by Bonaventure (d. 1274), whose work had a profound and lasting influence, not just on Franciscans but on all later medieval authors who wrote on the Passion." See Thomas H. Bestul, *Texts of the Passion: Latin Devotional Literature and Medieval Society*

Remembering and Responding to the Passion

A large portion of Franciscan spirituality and theology is oriented around the life and religious experience of St. Francis of Assisi, the charismatic founder of our order. Not only was Francis's great devotion to the Passion of the Lord Jesus Christ seen in the Office of the Passion that he authored, a liturgical text to be used by friars in praying the Divine Office that stressed meditation on the suffering of the Lord, but it was also captured in the great mystical experience of 1224, when after spending a period of prayer and fasting on the Franciscan holy mountain of Mount La Verna, Francis experienced a vision of a six-winged seraphic angel appearing in the form of the Crucified Christ, which resulted in him receiving the stigmata wounds on his body. On his hands, feet, and side, Francis of Assisi received the supernatural wounds of the Crucifixion, becoming in his flesh a living icon of the Passion of Christ.

This mystical experience is described by the preeminent historian of Western Christian mysticism Bernard McGinn as "the most famous experience of identification with the passion of Christ in the history of Christian mysticism,"[3] allowing Francis to be represented as "the mystic *par excellence*, the one rapt into unique union with the suffering Christ."[4] It was later depicted in poetry, painting, sculpture, iconography, hymns, biographies,

---

(Philadelphia, PA: University of Pennsylvania Press, 1996), 43; see also, for the Franciscan influence on the devotion, pp. 43–56.

[3] Bernard McGinn dedicated his third volume in his multivolume history on mysticism to the influence of Francis of Assisi and Franciscan spirituality on the Christian mystical tradition, among other influences. See Bernard McGinn, *The Flowering of Mysticism: Men and Women in the New Mysticism—1200–1350*, vol. 3 (New York: Crossroad, 1994). The cited note comes from an introductory "Note on the Cover Illustration" on an opening page that is not numbered and makes reference in terms of the cover illustration to a panel depicting Francis receiving the stigmata painted by the medieval Italian artist Giotto di Bondone (ca. 1266–1337).

[4] McGinn, *The Flowering of Mysticism*, 42.

hagiographies, and devotional books that permeated the imagination of European devotion. What was emphasized here, and became especially significant in terms of the influence of St. Francis, was moving medieval devotion to a concentration on the humanity of Jesus, specifically the suffering humanity of Jesus, how He suffered in His poverty and Crucifixion. Francis the stigmatic became a living icon that guided souls toward the poor and crucified Jesus, influencing deeper devotion to the Passion.

Previously, in the early Middle Ages, there was a general trend in spirituality and devotion of seeing Christ as the great Cosmic Judge. While that expression certainly contains truth, it is but one layer of a more multidimensional mosaic that constitutes the holistic beauty of who Jesus is in His sacred identity. The problem with accentuating that one side of Christ, as the great Cosmic Judge, is that it can lead to a spiritual and emotional distance in the relationship. The Christian soul can be drawn to moral living through the fear of hell or punishment, but that is rudimentary spirituality at best and it is difficult to sustain, as it is living out of a sense of obligation and not out of a sense of love, which should be the goal that truly inflames the human heart to depths of devotion and ongoing conversion.

Certainly, we cannot ignore the reality of God as judge, for judgment and eternal consequences for our moral and spiritual decisions are real. Any expression of Christianity that wants to pretend otherwise—pretending that sin is not real and that our actions do not have consequences; therefore, we can do whatever we want—is a farce and a mockery of the Cross, since Jesus died to save us from sin. But the Christian soul is, at its core, called to a deeper spirituality which draws the soul to pursuing excellence in the moral and spiritual life through an intense and radical love affair with Jesus Christ, through crucified love. That is to say, the judgment of God is a reality, but it should be the secondary factor and not the primary one that moves the soul to act. My desire for heaven should be based not on the benefits that I receive but on Him whom I love and want to receive. The love that the soul expresses, its entire life of self-gift, must be a response to the ultimate act of Love which was offered at Calvary. To contemplate Jesus Crucified, to meditate on His Passion, His immense suffering, His spiritual, emotional, and physical anguish, and to realize that it was all given for you, is to contemplate true Love.

There is a classic work of medieval Franciscan spirituality known as the *Sacred Exchange between St. Francis and Lady Poverty*. Scholars are not sure who the author is, but one suggestion, among others, is that it may have been St. Anthony of Padua or the Franciscan reformer and spiritual writer Ubertino da Casale. The *Sacred Exchange* is an allegory that tells the story of St. Francis and his friars climbing a mountain in order to reach Lady Poverty. The image of scaling a mountain symbolizes spiritual ascent and the image, in the Franciscan tradition, of being betrothed to Lady Poverty symbolizes a friar who is living his religious life well— especially through poverty, prayer, and penance—being a faithful son of St. Francis.

When Francis and his friars reach Lady Poverty, she explains that many friars and religious have abandoned her and no longer want her as a spouse, for they find her (and, specifically, the life she offers) too demanding. There are other followers of Christ, however, who throughout the ages, succeeding the Apostles, have still remained faithful to her, Lady Poverty explains.

What is the difference between these religious, the faithful and the unfaithful?

Lady Poverty explains that the truth about her teachings on a radically holy life and all its demands "remained among many for a long time, especially as long as the blood of the poor Crucified was still warm in their memory and the wonderful cup of his suffering inebriated their hearts."[5] In fact, she continues,

---

[5] "The Sacred Exchange between Saint Francis and Lady Poverty," in *Francis of Assisi: Early Documents*, vol. I, *The Saint*, ed. Regis J. Armstrong, J. A.

if there were any who were tempted to abandon her and the way of life she offered, "as they remembered the Lord's wounds which revealed the bowels of piety, they would punish themselves severely for this temptation, cling to me more strongly, and embrace me more fervently. Therefore I was always with them, deepening the sorrows of their memories of the eternal King's suffering."[6]

The keys here underlying this rich Franciscan text and its spirituality are "memory" and the Passion of Christ. Notice the perpetual emphasis on the power of memory: "As long as the blood of the poor Crucified was still warm in their memory . . . as they remembered the Lord's wounds . . . I was always with them, deepening the sorrows of their memories of the eternal King's suffering." What Lady Poverty is essentially articulating is that religious who were constantly recalling the memory of the Lord's suffering and Crucifixion, constantly meditating upon the Passion in their minds, had a *Why* that inspired them to live out greater lives of sacrificial devotion. They were inspired by the love of Jesus during His Passion, how much He endured for them, and they were able to respond to that love with their own expression of sacrificial love.

If the Lord suffered horrible torture, humiliation, and death for me, then I can fast today, and I can give more to prayer, and I can lead a poor, austere, simple life honoring His sacrifice. This type of spirituality was meant to be not only a response to the Passion but also an interior participation in the Passion. That interior participation in the Passion had both a Christocentric and a Marian emphasis. Let us turn to the Marian dimension.

Wayne Hellmann, and William J. Short (Hyde Park, NY: New City Press, 1999), 540.

[6] Francis of Assisi, "The Sacred Exchange," 540.

Sharing in Her Sufferings

What was especially highlighted in relation to Our Lady was the desire to share emotionally and spiritually in her sufferings at the foot of the Cross. This "sharing" was pursued through meditation. The medieval Franciscan mystic St. Angela of Foligno writes of her experience: "[In meditating] I entered into the sorrow over the Passion suffered by the mother of Christ and St. John. I prayed that they would obtain for me a sure sign by which I might always keep the Passion of Christ continually in my memory."[7]

Perhaps no other work has more beautifully and poetically expressed this spirituality of sharing in Our Lady's sorrows at the foot of the Cross than the thirteenth-century hymn *Stabat Mater*, considered one of the greatest hymns of Latin Christianity. Although there has been some scholarly debate about who the true author of the *Stabat Mater* is, for the longest time (and most Catholic hymnal books still recognize this sentiment when crediting authorship) the verses were attributed to the great medieval Franciscan poet and mystic Jacopone da Todi (1230–1306).

We are most accustomed today to hearing the *Stabat Mater* sung during the praying of the Stations of the Cross, especially during the season of Lent. The hauntingly beautiful lyrics of the hymn become an invitation for us to enter internally into the sufferings of Mother Mary's sorrows as she contemplates the pains of her crucified Son. The first half of the *Stabat Mater* begins with emphasizing those sorrows. Stanza 2 poetically connects her suffering to Simeon's prophecy as it reflects how she shared in Christ's anguish:

> Through her heart, his sorrow sharing,
> All his bitter anguish bearing,
> now at length the sword has passed.

---

[7] *Angela of Foligno: Complete Works*, ed. and trans. Paul Lechance (Mahwah, NJ: 1993), 128.

Stanza 7 enters into the core of the anguish experienced, capturing how it is the pain of a mother that is being witnessed here, the unbearable pain of a mother watching her child in torment:

> Bruised, derided, cursed, defiled,
> She beheld her tender Child
> All with bloody scourges rent.

There is a transition that is made from stanza 9 and onwards to the first person singular, the voice of the narrator speaking on our behalf, as we feel ourselves immersed into the drama of the Passion and the personal desire of sharing in the intimacy of our sorrowful Mother's pain. "Make me feel as thou hast felt" (stanza 10):

> Holy Mother! pierce me through,
> In my heart each wound renew
> Of my Savior crucified.

In these meaningful verses there is the paradox of the *honor of suffering* with Jesus and Mary:

> Let me mingle tears with thee,
> Mourning Him who mourned for me,
> All the days that I may live.

> By the cross with thee to stay;
> There with thee to weep and pray,
> Is all I ask of thee to give.[8]

---

[8] All of the above stanzas are taken from Jacopone da Todi, "At the Cross Her Station Keeping" (*Stabat Mater Dolorosa*), in *Breaking Bread 2019*, trans. Edward Caswall (Portland, OR: OCP, 2018), no. 120.

The honor of suffering with Jesus and Mary brings an intense joy to the innermost depths of the soul. It is a paradox that only a supernatural vision of life can comprehend, that there is bliss that such shared sorrow can evoke in the soul. It sounds like the most sublime irony, but it is a reality of the spiritual life, of a spirituality of crucified love.

"There is joy also in sorrow, and it is a very pure joy," Fr. Neubert writes. "There is infinitely more happiness in weeping with Mary at the foot of the cross, in uniting our sufferings with those of Jesus and the *Mater Dolorosa*, than in rejoicing with the fortunate ones of this world. With Paul, we who are united to Mary will be able to say that we 'exceedingly abound with joy in all our tribulation.'"[9]

It is asking for an interior experience of the Passion that is, at its heart, painful, but sees the experience of sharing suffering as a form of intimacy and union. There is, after all, no greater act of love than to suffer for the one that you love. Here "sharing suffering" means that we bring our own pains and poverty to the foot of the Cross, our own struggles and difficulties that life has brought us, and we say to Jesus and Mary, "Here is my gift. The gift of my poverty, of my sufferings. I offer them in union with your sufferings. Let us suffer together, my beloved ones." It is a paradox of the mystical life. Sometimes it is the person who is suffering more who can offer Jesus and Mary a greater gift, an encounter in the most vulnerable places where only those who are undergoing trial can enter: Gethsemane and Calvary. These are the interior places of deepest intimacy, where the blood of Christ meets our own blood, where Our Lady's tears meet our tears. It is in our poverty wherein the Crucified Jesus and the Mother of Sorrows meet us most intimately. Here we experience a personal immersion into the heart of the Passion, and it becomes one of the highest forms

---

[9] Fr. Emile Neubert, *Life of Union with Mary* (New Bedford, MA: Academy of the Immaculate, 2014), 101.

of love. Here our wounds meet their wounds, and united with those of Jesus and Mary, our wounds become transformed, suffering leads to intimacy, an expansion of the heart that changes us from within and allows us depths of relationship that comfort could never provide.

"They Have Killed both Mother and Son"

Jacopone da Todi, whether or not he is the actual author of the *Stabat Mater*, possessed a spiritual theology in his writings that, epitomizing the medieval Franciscan spirit, stressed the unique quality of Our Lady's sufferings in union with Jesus at Calvary. Jacopone's *Lauds*, a collection of his poems, hymns, dramatic dialogues, and letters, makes this reality clear. In the final laud, Jacopone presents a poetic dialogue between Jesus and Mary at the Crucifixion:

> Mother, why have you come?
> Your agony and tears crush Me;
> To see you suffer so will be My death.[10]

Here Jacopone captures a special quality, one that is seldom mentioned, about Jesus's sufferings at Calvary: the paradox that the presence of Mary brings. "Paradox" because, on the one hand, her presence constitutes a drop of unconditional love among an ocean of hatred that surrounds Him, offering the consolation of pure love. On the other hand, her presence may offer Jesus His greatest distress because—among the shouts of anger and mockery, among the blasphemies, among His own physical torture and interior anguish, among the utter humiliation and devastation that is the Crucifixion—He needs to see His Mother's pain, and to see her hurt so much constitutes a greater affliction for Him

---

[10] Jacopone da Todi, *The Lauds*, trans. Serge Hughes and Elizabeth Hughes (New York: Paulist Press, 1982), 280.

than His own suffering, her hurt becoming a part of His suffering, perhaps the heaviest part to bear.

Poignantly does Jacopone capture Mary's sufferings in witnessing Jesus die, invoking her voice as he writes:

> Why did the world so despise You?
> Gentle and sweet Son, Son of a sorrowful mother,
> How cruelly You have been treated!
> ... The sword they prophesied has pierced my heart.
> They have killed both mother and son,
> One cruel death for both,
> Embracing each other and their common cross![11]

When Jacopone writes, from Mary's perspective, "Why did the world so despise You? / Gentle and sweet Son," we begin to perceive the pain of a mother mourning for her innocent and pure child, a child so mistreated and abused by what the world had to offer. To try to even come close to understanding the interior depths of Mother Mary's sufferings, of the sword piercing her heart, it is important to see that, for her, she is not just witnessing the Crucifixion of Jesus as God-Man, but she is witnessing the Crucifixion of her beloved, innocent child, whom she gave birth to, nourished, and has loved affectionately like no one else for most of her life. Deeply personal is the interior sorrow of this poor, afflicted mother.

An anonymous fourteenth-century English lyric captures this reality poignantly, through the perspective of Mother Mary's voice:

> Why do you not have any pity on my child?
> Have pity on me, full of mourning,
> Take my precious child down from the Cross,
> Or impale me on the Cross together with my darling.

---

[11] Jacopone da Todi, *The Lauds*, 280.

I could not have been subjected to a bigger torment
Than being left to live in sorrow and in shame.
Since love binds me with my son,
Let us die both together.[12]

Similar to Jacopone's emphasis of "one cruel death for both," this English work speaks to Jesus and Mary dying together. It is a reality that even Pope St. John Paul II acknowledged, reflecting once that at Calvary, watching Jesus's physical Crucifixion, Mary had to endure a spiritual crucifixion. "Crucified spiritually with her crucified Son (cf. Gal 2:20), she contemplated with heroic love the death of her God."[13] What is being recognized here is the intimate spiritual union of the Sacred Heart with the Immaculate Heart. When one is cut, the other bleeds with it—hence, one cannot experience a crucifixion without the other; their souls are too intimately united.

It was Jacopone's contemporary, the great medieval Franciscan theologian, philosopher, minister general of the Franciscan order, and cardinal of the Church St. Bonaventure of Bagnoregio (1221–1274), who wrote some of the most poignantly eloquent expressions of Mother Mary's sorrow, mourning her child as she is witnessing His Crucifixion. In his spiritual treatise *The Tree of Life*, Bonaventure wrote:

> What tongue can tell, what intellect grasp the heavy weight of your desolation, blessed Virgin? You were present at all these events, standing close by and participating in them in every way. This blessed and most holy

---

[12] As quoted in Eva De Visscher, "Marian Devotion in the Latin West in the Later Middle Ages," in *Mary: The Complete Resource*, ed. Sarah Jane Boss (New York: Oxford University Press, 2007), 184.

[13] As quoted in Msgr. Arthur Burton Calkins, "Mary: Co-redemptrix: The Beloved Associate of Christ," 397. John Paul II's words are taken from a homily that he gave on January 31, 1985, at the Shrine of Our Lady of the Dawn in Guayaquil, Ecuador.

flesh—which you so chastely conceived, so sweetly nourished and fed with your milk, which you so often held on
your lap, and kissed with your lips—you actually gazed
upon with your bodily eyes now torn by the blows of the
scourges, now pierced by the points of the thorns, now
struck by the reed, now beaten by the hands and fists,
now pierced by nails and fixed to the wood of the cross,
and torn by its own weight as it hung there, now mocked
in every way, finally made to drink gall and vinegar.[14]

Bonaventure's heart-rending juxtaposition, presenting side by side
the flesh of the Child Jesus that was nourished, fed, and kissed by
Our Lady now being torn by the scourges, pierced by nails, and
mocked in every way, presents the emotional appeal to grasping
the pain of a mother.

What Bonaventure is doing here is exactly what the filmmaker
Mel Gibson did centuries later with his 2004 masterpiece film *The
Passion of the Christ*. The iconic scene that especially speaks to the
heart, in its aching beauty, is the scene wherein Mary witnesses
from a distance Jesus fall to the ground underneath the heaviness
of the Cross, an angry and violent crowd surrounding Him. In
the midst of witnessing the fall, Mother Mary's mind instanta-
neously experiences a nostalgic flashback, a scene from Jesus's
childhood wherein He fell and she ran to Him, lovingly helping
her child up and embracing Him in maternal consolation. Now,
the teary-eyed Mother, seeing her child fall again, once again runs
toward Him, to embrace Him and tell Him that beyond all the
evil that surrounds Him, she is here. Notwithstanding the cruel
and enraged crowds, notwithstanding the violent scourging of the
Roman soldiers, notwithstanding the stones that are thrown at
Him and the hatred that is shouted at Him, she still runs toward

---

[14] *Bonaventure: The Soul's Journey into God, the Tree of Life, the Life of St. Francis*,
trans. Ewert Cousins (New York: Paulist Press, 1978), 152–53.

Him because she is led by love, by a love that is unconditional and that is willing to undertake any sacrifice for Him. It doesn't matter to her whether she is trampled by the crowed; it doesn't matter to her whether she is verbally abused or humiliated by the malice that possesses people; she is led by love and will go through any danger and any evil to comfort her beloved Son.

During one period of his life as a Franciscan friar, Bonaventure served as Master of Novices. In a work that he addressed to his novices on the topic of prayer, summarizing the spiritual wisdom of St. Bernard of Clairvaux, Bonaventure teaches his novices how to meditate upon the Passion of Christ. For Bonaventure, as for many medieval spiritual writers, the vivid and visual usage of the imagination is paramount to entering deeper immersion into the sufferings of Christ.

> Picture the bloody sweat, the outrageous blows, the stinging lashes, the thorny crown, the blasphemous spit, the mocking words, the weighty cross. Picture him hanging from the cross, the bloodshot eyes, the pallid lips, the gall and vinegar, the bowed head, the agony of death. No need for more! Life itself has died for us! And when you have meditated on these things for some time, return again to yourself and consider that Christ suffered not only these but many other torments to free you from the devil's slavery.[15]

Here Bonaventure is being true to—and, in fact, being a key representative of—that medieval Franciscan tradition that stressed

---

[15] Bonaventure, "Instructions to Novices: Prayer," in *Works of Saint Bonaventure: Writings Concerning the Franciscan Order*, ed. and trans. Dominic Monti, OFM (St. Bonaventure, NY: Franciscan Institute of St. Bonaventure University, 1994), 155. Whereas Bonaventure has these words in quotation marks, introducing them as the words of Bernard of Clairvaux, Dominic Monti explains that this "is not an exact quotation, but the sentiments are very common in Bernard" (155n35).

the importance of daily remembering and meditating upon the Passion. For Bonaventure at least two components are incredibly important.

First, having a vivid, visual mental picture of the sufferings of Christ—the more prominent the imagery, the more easily is it internalized and stimulates the spiritual senses. Second, it is important to connect the meditation upon the Passion to one's own life, to bring it back to oneself and realize that these torments, and many others, were endured by Christ for the sake of one's salvation. It is, essentially, a sacrificial act of love that is deeply personal.

Re-Crucifying Christ

What is important to recognize is that this spirituality which highlights the Passion is not a spirituality that should be relegated to the medieval past but one whose awareness needs to reach the consciousness of Christians in the present day. The Passion is an event that, while of paramount historical importance and which took place in first-century Palestine, transcends time and has continual consequences. Consider the wisdom of two Church-approved apparitions on this matter.

Our Lady in her 1846 apparitions in La Salette, France, gave a disturbingly powerful message wherein she expressed that "the ministers of my Son, the priests by their wicked lives, by their irreverence and their impiety in the celebration of the holy mysteries, by their love of money, their love of honors and pleasures, the priests have become cesspools of impurity. . . . Woe to the priests and those dedicated to God who by their infidelity and their wicked lives are crucifying My Son again!"[16]

---

[16] "Messages of the Apparitions: La Salette, France 1846," The Miracle Hunter, accessed January 15, 2022, http://www.miraclehunter.com/marian_apparitions/messages/lasalette_messages2.html.

This is a very troubling and severe message but, of course, in light of the tragedy of the priestly abuse scandals that have become public in recent decades, among other scandals within the clergy, these revelations of Our Lady of La Salette, as intrinsically disturbing as they are, no longer seem so difficult to believe. The clergy, because of the gift of our special conformity to the person of Christ, *in persona Christi*, have an even greater responsibility toward living out lives of holiness, purity, austerity, and prayer. Of course, that does not dismiss the important role that the laity play nor the responsibility that many lay men and women have, as well, in crucifying Jesus. All of our sins crucify Him, and the ways that we sin correspond to the ways that He had to suffer. Because of our sins of the flesh, for example, He had to suffer unmercifully in His flesh, particularly the horrible scourging.

In a disturbing but illuminating revelation of the Passion, St. Faustina was shown the following vision while praying during nocturnal adoration on a Thursday night:

> When I came for adoration, an inner recollection took hold of me immediately, and I saw the Lord Jesus tied to a pillar, stripped of His clothes, and the scourging began immediately. I saw four men who took turns at striking the Lord with scourges. My heart almost stopped at the sight of these tortures. The Lord said to me, **I suffer even greater pain than that which you see.** And Jesus gave me to know for what sins He subjected himself to the scourging: these are sins of impurity. Oh, how dreadful was Jesus' moral suffering during the scourging! Then Jesus said to me, **Look and see the human race in its present condition.** In an instant, I saw horrible things: the executioners left Jesus, and other people started scourging Him; they seized the scourges and struck the Lord mercilessly. These were priests, religious men and women; and high dignitaries of the Church, which

surprised me greatly. There were lay people of all ages and walks of life. All vented their malice on the innocent Jesus. Seeing this, my heart fell as if into a mortal agony.[17]

How significant are the Lord's words in this revelation when He tells St. Faustina, "Look and see the human race in its present condition." What this reality tells us is that when we choose sin, especially sins of impurity, we are not simply violating abstract moral codes of behavior—no, it is more personal. With our sins of the flesh, we are crucifying and scourging Jesus in the flesh. He is so intimately intertwined with us, the mystical body, as the Head of the Church, that when we sin, He feels it.

Lest one falls into the temptation of thinking that this type of Passion spirituality, highlighting that Jesus still suffers in His Passion because of our sins, is simply the fanciful construction of private revelations and not grounded in the deposit of faith, it is noteworthy to consider that both Scripture and papal teachings, thus the magisterial tradition, also emphasize this spirituality and its importance.

The assumption may be that because Jesus already suffered and died on the Cross, was resurrected, ascended into heaven, and exists in eternal beatitude, He no longer suffers—or that He no longer can suffer. The reality, however, is that Jesus and Mary, as Head of the mystical body and Mother of the mystical body, still can suffer, especially through the Church.

The Letter to the Hebrews speaks of members of the Church who initially had accepted the Christian mysteries but later fell away from the faith, rejecting it with the sin of apostasy; thus explaining: "They crucify the Son of God on their own account and hold him up to contempt" (Heb 6:6). This is articulated as

---

[17] St. Faustina Maria Kowalska, *Divine Mercy in My Soul: Diary of Saint Maria Faustina Kowalska* (Stockbridge, MA: Marian Press, 2011), no. 445.

a present-tense reality, years after His historical Crucifixion on Calvary.

Similarly, on his road-to-Damascus encounter with Christ, when Saul experiences a flash of light and falls to the ground, he "heard a voice saying to him, 'Saul, Saul, why do you persecute me?' And he said, 'Who are you, Lord?' And he said, 'I am Jesus, whom you are persecuting'" (Acts 9:4–5). Here we see how Jesus, after His Resurrection and Ascension, still mystically suffers through the sins committed against His Church. As Head of the mystical body, Christ suffers in His Church, in the sufferings of her members and through the sins of those who persecute the Church.

Pope Pius XI wrote about this matter in his encyclical on reparation to the Sacred Heart *Miserentissimus Redemptor*, in which he comments on the experience of Saul on the road to Damascus, writing that the words of Christ signify "that when persecutions are stirred up against the Church, the Divine Head of the Church is Himself attacked and troubled. Rightly, therefore, does Christ, still suffering in His mystical body, desire to have us partakers of His expiation, and this is also demanded by our intimate union with Him, for since we are 'the body of Christ and members of member' (1 *Corinthians* xii, 27), whatever the head suffers, all the members must suffer with it (Cf. 1 *Corinthians* xii, 26)."[18]

Pius XI expounds on this point, powerfully highlighting how each sin "in its own way" renews the Passion of Christ. He articulates that "the sins of men and their crimes committed in every age were the cause why Christ was delivered up to death, and now also they would of themselves bring death to Christ, joined with the same griefs and sorrows, since each . . . sin in its own way is held to renew the passion of Our Lord: 'Crucifying again to themselves the Son of God, and making him a mockery' (*Hebrews* vi, 6)."[19]

Because of the reality that the Passion of the Lord is renewed,

---

[18] Pope Pius XI, Encyclical Letter *Miserentissimus Redemptor* (1928), §14.

[19] Pius XI, *Miserentissimus Redemptor*, §13.

there is a spirituality that we Christians can participate in which offers reparation and consolation to Jesus's Sacred Heart for these continual offenses that He suffers:

> Now if, because of our sins also which were as yet in the future, but were foreseen, the soul of Christ became sorrowful unto death, it cannot be doubted that then, too, already He derived somewhat of solace from our reparation, which was likewise foreseen, when "there appeared to Him an angel from heaven" (*Luke* xxii, 43), in order that His Heart, oppressed with weariness and anguish, might find consolation.[20]

Here Pius XI, akin to accounts written by mystics who have reported seeing the Lord's sufferings in Gethsemane, inspirationally articulates that when Jesus underwent His agony in the Garden and, according to the Gospel of Luke, an angel of light came to Him to offer consolation, the angel showed Him all those persons who, throughout the centuries, would live for Him and offer reparation to Jesus as an act of love and consolation against the ingratitude and sins of humanity that He must endure.[21] Pius XI goes on to express that now we have an opportunity to be those who consoled Him when He suffered in Gethsemane, and

---

[20] Pius XI, *Miserentissimus Redemptor*, §13.

[21] Pius XI explains that in order to make reparation, "there have been established many religious families of men and women whose purpose it is by earnest service, both by day and by night, in some manner to fulfill the office of the Angel consoling Jesus in the garden; hence come certain associations of pious men, approved by the Apostolic See and enriched with indulgences, who take upon themselves this same duty of making expiation, a duty which is to be fulfilled by fitting exercises of devotion and of the virtues; hence lastly, to omit other things, come the devotions and solemn demonstrations for the purpose of making reparation to the offended Divine honor, which are inaugurated everywhere, not only by pious members of the faithful, but by parishes, dioceses and cities." *Miserentissimus Redemptor*, §19.

continue to console Him as His Sacred Heart is offended by so much ingratitude. "And so even now, in a wondrous yet true manner, we can and ought to console that Most Sacred Heart which is continually wounded by the sins of thankless men."[22]

Why is it so important to revive such a spirituality for today, a spirituality focused on the suffering of Jesus and Mary?

One major reason is given by Our Lady during her apparitions at Fatima. That reason, identical to Pius XI highlighting "the sins of thankless men," points to the ingratitude of humanity and the need to make reparations to the Sacred and Immaculate Hearts of Jesus and Mary in order to make up for the sins of humanity and for our own sins. Here we enter another dimension of Marian spirituality that is highly significant and essential to developing a deeper relationship with her: a spirituality of reparation.

This is a beautiful spirituality that is connected to the Mother of Sorrows, as it tries to console our Mother in her current sorrow, a sorrow that is an extension of seeing her Son crucified. She suffers with Him, as her Immaculate Heart is intimately united to His Sacred Heart. In a following chapter we will explore in greater detail how we can make reparation and offer consolation to these precious, suffering Hearts. But before we do, let us contemplate even deeper the topic of Our Lady's sufferings with Jesus, turning to a matter that mystics have acknowledged in their revelations, and that theology and Scripture may indeed support: the possibility that the Virgin Mary experienced the interior stigmata during Christ's Passion.

---

[22] Pius XI, *Miserentissimus Redemptor*, §13.

Chapter 5

THE STIGMATA OF MARY?

Insights from the Mystical and Theological Tradition

I have already mentioned in other places of this history, and especially in that of the Passion, that the blessed Mother felt in her own body the torments of her Son. This was true also of the scourging, which She felt in all the parts of her virginal body, in the same intensity as they were felt by Christ in His body.

—Venerable Maria of Ágreda, *Mystical City of God*

And a sword will pierce through your own soul also.

—Simeon to Mary, Luke 2:35

There is a fascinating, yet little known, tradition in the visionary literature of Christian mystics that depicts Our Lady as the first stigmatic. A number of mystics who have reported experiencing visions and revelations of the life of Jesus and Mary in first-century Palestine have recorded, in their visionary literature, a mystical grace that Our Lady apparently received during the Passion of her Son, Jesus. She began to feel the pains that His body was enduring, from the scourges, to the blows, to the crown of thorns, and nails. Historically, it is St. Francis of Assisi who is acknowledged as the first *recorded* stigmatic in Christianity, though there have been debates about the possibility of earlier stigmata cases; and it is certainly not beyond the realm of possibility that, during His Passion, Jesus's mother may have shared internally in the sufferings of her Son through invisible stigmata. One could argue that on a theological level it would even be fitting.

To come to a greater appreciation of Mother Mary's love for Jesus and the potential depths of her suffering, let us explore this interesting possibility, starting with how vividly it is depicted in the revelations of a prominent Marian mystic and venerable.

Insights from the Mystical City of God

The Venerable Maria of Ágreda (1602–1665) was a Spanish nun and mystic who during her life reported experiencing various mystical phenomena from God, among them Eucharistic ecstasies, levitations, bilocation, the ability to read souls, and visions and revelations of the life of the Virgin Mary. Interestingly, Maria of Ágreda even had a distant but direct influence in helping the Church to solemnly define the dogma of the Immaculate Conception centuries later in 1854. She established a spiritual friendship with King Philip IV of Spain, who was fascinated with Sister Maria and her mystical experiences and writings and exchanged over six hundred letters with her over a twenty-two-year period. Within those letters, Sister Maria strongly encouraged the king to use his influence to approach two successive popes, Innocent X and Alexander VII, in order to support the Immaculate Conception, the reality that Our Lady was preserved from the stain of original sin from the first moment of her conception.[1] The dogma was yet to be promulgated, yet the reality of the dogma as a sacred truth about Our Lady was strongly present in the revelations that Sister Maria received from the Virgin Mary.

Making it a state affair, King Philip engaged a number of

---

[1] See Marilyn H. Fedewa, *María of Ágreda: Mystical Lady in Blue* (Albuquerque, NM: University of New Mexico Press, 2009), 100–103. A more recent biographical work by the same author: Marilyn H. Fedewa, *Dark Eyes, Lady Blue: María of Ágreda* (Lubbock, TX: Texas Tech University Press, 2020).

learned theologians on the matter and appointed ambassadors to the pope, while sending copious documentation in support of the Immaculate Conception. On December 8, 1661, Pope Alexander VII released a decree supporting the Immaculate Conception, and nearly two centuries later, on December 8, 1854, Pope Pius IX released the apostolic constitution *Ineffabilis Deus*, in which he solemnly defined the dogma of the Immaculate Conception of the Blessed Virgin Mary. Within the text, he cited Alexander VII's 1661 papal bull in support of the Immaculate Conception, which credited the influence of King Philip IV of Spain for his advocacy of the dogma, implicitly acknowledging Venerable Maria of Ágreda's influence. "So at the instance and request of the bishops mentioned above, with the chapters of the churches, and of King Philip and his kingdoms, we renew the Constitutions and Decrees issued by the Roman Pontiffs, our predecessors . . . in favor of the doctrine asserting that the soul of the Blessed Virgin, in its creation and infusion into the body, was endowed with the grace of the Holy Spirit and preserved from original sin."[2]

Maria of Ágreda's revelations of the life of Mary were recorded in a multivolume text known as the *Mystical City of God*, the first edition itself constituting about 2,700 pages. Today, the *Mystical City of God* is known as a treasure of mystical literature and is a classic of Spanish Mariology. One of the most powerful sections of the work depicts the Passion of the Lord Jesus Christ and the unique participation that Jesus's mother had in her special communion with Him in His Passion.

Maria of Ágreda writes about Our Lady's prayer during the

---

[2] Alexander VII, quoted in Pius IX, *Ineffabilis Deus* (1854). Marilyn Fedewa explains that to "this day, Marian scholars credit Sor María of Ágreda and King Felipe IV with favorably influencing Alexander VII on the doctrine. . . . Alexander VII's 1661 decree is considered the turning point in the evolution of the Immaculate Conception. Many consider it the definitive statement on the doctrine until it was fully established by Pope Pius IX in 1854." See Fedewa, *María of Ágreda*, 100.

Passion, how beginning with Holy Thursday a radically loving request was made by the Mother of God. "She begged the eternal Father to suspend in Her all human alleviation and comfort, both in the sensitive and in the spiritual part of Her being, so that nothing might hinder Her from suffering to the highest degree in union with her divine Son. She prayed that She might be permitted to feel and participate in her virginal body all the pains of the wounds and tortures about to be undergone by Jesus."[3] The text continues to explain that this special request of the Virgin Mary was granted to her by God, and, therefore, "the Mother in consequence suffered all the torments of her most holy Son in exact duplication" during the Passion.[4]

Notice two important aspects of the torments that Mary suffered, according to the *Mystical City of God*. She requested, first, in her prayer, to suffer on an interior (that is, spiritual-emotional) level of complete darkness and desolation. Here there is a beautiful communion that she desired to experience with Jesus's dark night of the soul. Jesus had to experience an interior anguish so severe and desolate, a felt spiritual abandonment of such abysmal misery, that at Calvary He yelled out, in unspeakable affliction, "My God, my God, why have you forsaken me?" (Matt 27:46). The heaviness of the interior weight that His soul had to carry was so severe, as He took the sins of the entire world upon Himself, that earlier in Gethsemane He started sweating blood.

Whether this phenomenon happened on a supernatural level or a natural level is a good question. If it was happening on a supernatural level, Jesus may have been experiencing the stigmata in a foreshadowing of His crowning with thorns, the regal crown and dress of the true King not being gold, in this case, but crimson red, His sacred blood. If it was happening on a natural

---

[3] Maria of Ágreda, *The Mystical City of God: A Popular Abridgement of the Divine History and Life of the Virgin Mother of God*, trans. Fiscar Marison (Charlotte, NC: TAN Books, 1978), 502.

[4] Maria of Ágreda, *Mystical City*, 502.

level, it speaks vividly to the unmatched immensity of the anxiety that His mind and soul absorbed in the spiritual and psychological heaviness that He had to endure, as it is a scientific fact that individuals who experience moments of severe stress in a trauma that may feel too overwhelming to bear can, at times, begin to sweat blood.

It is also important to note that these categories—of natural and supernatural—are not always exclusive since a powerful experience can constitute an integration of the two, as a human person is a composite of mind, soul, and body. Hence, the mind may be psychologically affected as the soul feels spiritually traumatized through an experience of desolate darkness, and the body may, in fact, manifest a physical reaction to these strong internal realities. Here we need to be careful with our language: carefully I write that the "soul *feels* spiritually traumatized" during an experience of darkness since in a genuine dark night of the soul what is in fact happening is a purification of the soul. It will feel like a traumatizing experience, spiritually speaking, but is in fact a purifying experience that cleanses the soul of its imperfections and absorbs it in great Light as the soul's dependency on God becomes complete.

However, in order to understand properly, on a spiritual and theological level, the experiences of Jesus and Mary during the Passion, it is important to grasp certain distinctions pertaining to spiritual theology, especially the dark nights that a soul can experience.

The Suffering of the Soul

Classical spiritual writers of the Christian tradition have acknowledged three main stages of ascent, or growth, in the spiritual life: the purgative, the illuminative, and the unitive. Between these stages there are, traditionally, two major dark nights that offer purification of the soul through periods of desolation and suffering:

(1) a dark night of the senses, which helps a soul advance from the purgative to the illuminative stage, and (2) a dark night of the soul (sometimes also called "the dark night of the spirit"), a much fiercer and severe abyss of spiritual darkness whose depths plunge a soul into complete poverty, the feeling of absolute abandonment by God, and a deep-seated spiritual cleansing of roots of imperfection that prepares the soul for transformative union with God.

Another way to understand these spiritual realities is through the language of prayer. In the earlier stage of the spiritual life, the purgative phase, prayer is usually vocal and meditative. As a person draws nearer to the illuminative stage, the predominant form of prayer becomes more contemplative, usually beginning as a type of acquired contemplation, wherein the mind (cooperating with grace) experiences a greater interior stillness and relies less on visualization (that is, meditation), simply desiring to be in the presence of the Beloved. A true extraordinary grace comes—a supernatural act that cannot be cultivated on our side but must come from God—when a person's spiritual life moves beyond acquired contemplation and experiences infused contemplation. This is the transition from the purgative to the illuminative stage, which is tangibly experienced by how different one's prayer becomes. Here, a person has officially advanced from what spiritual theologians call ascetical prayer to mystical prayer.

Mystical prayer begins when God becomes the primary mover; in other words, it is no longer the person who initiates with spiritual exercises, but there is, as Fr. Antonio Royo Marin, O.P., writes, an "invasion of the soul by the supernatural," wherein God is experientially infusing a special grace of contemplation that is felt in the soul, leading the prayer. "When it is produced, the soul feels in an unmistakable and ineffable manner that it is invaded and permeated with something which it cannot describe in precision, but which the soul feels clearly as something supernatural. It is, in fact, an effect of the operation of the gifts of the Holy Ghost, which inundate the soul with supernatural life."[5]

What is an interesting and little-known fact is that the dark nights a person experiences on the spiritual journey already constitute experiences of infused contemplation. That is to say, if a person is experiencing a genuine dark night—whether that is a dark night of the senses or a dark night of the soul—that is an experience of mystical purging that is being infused into the soul by God. It sounds like a paradox, and certainly feels like one since, when a person is experiencing a dark night, the interior feelings are of emptiness, desolation, an abysmal void—as if God has left and abandoned the soul.

The opposite is the reality.

Not only has God not "left" but He is, in fact, more present by infusing the feelings of darkness that purify the soul and allow it to grow in dependency on God and in the virtues of faith, hope, and love, which are tested and strengthened when consolations are no longer the driving force behind a person's life of faith. True love is tested *and strengthened* (if one perseveres) during difficult times. This purifying experience also allows the soul not to become too attached to consolations. Yes, when the Lord allows and gives consolations, they are good and there is nothing wrong with delighting in His sweetness, His consolations being a loving caress expressing that sweetness. But the soul may also experience the temptation of becoming too attached to the consolations, or even feeling prideful for receiving them. Desolation, therefore, has its place. It can help purify a person's faith, reorienting it to a more sincere love of God and a deeper humility, once a soul realizes its poverty and absolute need for God.

---

[5] Antonio Royo Marin, O.P., *The Theology of Christian Perfection*, trans. Jordan Aumann, O.P. (Eugene, OR: Wipf & Stock, 2011), 532. Based on his doctoral dissertation, this work by Fr. Marin, a Spanish Dominican, is one of the most in-depth and precise textbooks ever written on the stages of the spiritual life and is his magnum opus on spiritual theology.

A further temptation that the soul can fall into is associating the presence of consolations with the presence of God and the absence of consolations with the absence of God. This is not always the case. As mentioned, when a person is experiencing a genuine dark night, then that experience constitutes an infusion of purifying grace—albeit, negatively felt—that signifies an expression of God's presence. In fact, the person who is experiencing a deep purging through a dark night may be more united to God and in a far more advanced spiritual state than a person who is experiencing consolations (and *feeling* closer to God) in an earlier state of the spiritual journey.

An important nuance about dark nights and desolations, however, needs to be understood. The question is this: Can feelings of desolation ever signify the absence of God?

Yes, they can. But here is the nuance: it happens when the desolation is the result of a person's sin. Mortal sin especially severs a right relationship with God and removes a soul from the state of grace. In that state of mortal sin, the soul will experience the absence of God through interior emptiness and desolation. It is important to understand that this type of darkness, however, is *not a genuine dark night of the senses or the soul*. A genuine dark night is an experience that comes when a person is growing in the spiritual life and when the Lord wants to take that person even deeper through a period of mystical purification. When we sin and experience the dark desolation of our own sinfulness, there is nothing mystical or purifying about that.

A life of sin leads to distance from God and an interior emptiness whose desolation may resemble the feelings of a dark night, but it is far from the mystically purifying dark night, whose depths bring us into hidden union with God through the burning crucible of love that He initiates. "There is no other path but through the burning love of the Crucified," as St. Bonaventure wrote in *The Soul's Journey into God.*[6]

What is very important to understand is that the darkness that Jesus and Mary experienced, especially during the Passion, would have a different end than the darkness experienced by mystics who have journeyed in their spiritual lives into the deeper realms of the night. As mentioned, authentic dark nights have the attribute of being purifying for the soul. Jesus and Mary would not need any purification, both being free of original and actual sin and thus completely pure. Therefore, their dark nights would have a distinctly redemptive character—suffering intended for the salvific redemption of souls—without the need for any type of personal purification.

But the heaviness of the darkness would still be experienced, especially as Christ bore the weight of the world's sins. In Gethsemane and on Calvary this interior abyss would reach its most heartbreaking culmination, as Jesus felt absolute abandonment from God the Father, crying out in inexpressible anguish to Him. Our Lady's night particularly would be offered in union with the Passion of Jesus in order to participate in a unique way in His one Redemption, no other person helping Jesus to save souls as singularly as she, the New Eve, did.[7]

---

[6] Bonaventure: *The Soul's Journey into God, the Tree of Life, the Life of St. Francis,* trans. Ewert Cousins (New York: Paulist Press, 1978), 54.

[7] "Predestined from eternity by that decree of divine providence which determined the incarnation of the Word to be the Mother of God, the Blessed Virgin was on this earth the virgin Mother of the Redeemer, and above all others and in a singular way the generous associate and humble handmaid of the Lord. She conceived, brought forth and nourished Christ. She presented Him to the Father in the temple, and was united with Him by compassion as He died on the Cross. In this singular way she cooperated by her obedience, faith, hope and burning charity in the work of the Saviour in giving back supernatural life to souls." Second Vatican Council, Dogmatic Constitution on the Church *Lumen Gentium* (1964), §61.

The Suffering of the Body

In addition to the sufferings that she requested on an interior, spiritual, and emotional level, Mother Mary also requested to suffer on a bodily level, to experience all the torments that Jesus would physically undergo. The request that Mary made for suffering with her Son is an act of intimacy because there is no greater act of love than to suffer with the one that you love. Otherwise, it would be a superficial and empty faith. Anyone can love another when times are good and pleasant. But it takes true love to be loyal and persevere when suffering enters; then it becomes a deeper intimacy, crucified love. Maria of Ágreda touches on the depths of the love that Our Lady had for Jesus and the sufferings that she was willing to endure for Him: "For in her most ardent love She would have considered it incomparably more painful to see her divine Son suffer and die without being allowed to share in his torments."[8]

Spiritually perceptive theologians of the Middle Ages have expressed similar sentiments in their homilies, poetry, and Passion treatises about Our Lady's sufferings. The medieval Cistercian Amadeus of Lausanne wrote, "She was more tortured than if she was suffering torture in herself, since she loved more than herself the source of her grief."[9] Similarly, his teacher and mentor, the great Cistercian theologian St. Bernard of Clairvaux, expressed in a homily, portions of which he addresses *to Our Lady* (a rhetorical device of a number of medieval preachers): "Therefore, a violent pain pierced your soul, so that we speak of you as more than a martyr. I am sure that for you, what you felt in sharing your Son's Passion was even worse than the sensation of physical suffering."[10]

---

[8] Maria of Ágreda, *Mystical City*, 502.

[9] As quoted in Eva De Visscher, "Marian Devotion in the Latin West in the Later Middle Ages," in *Mary: The Complete Resource*, ed. Sarah Jane Boss (New York: Oxford University Press, 2007), 183.

[10] As quoted in Robert Fastiggi, "Lessons from the Sermons of St. Bernard of Clairvaux," *The Priest*, July 15, 2020, https://www.thepriest.com/2020/07/15/lessons-from-the-sermons-of-st-bernard-of-clairvaux/.

Both Cistercian thinkers emphasize an enlightened understanding, a deep-seated truth that must come from the depths of
their contemplative lives, often the greatest source of wisdom. It is
the truth that the interior trauma that Mother Mary experienced
during her Son's Passion, the emotional and spiritual darkness that
pierced her soul, was far greater than were she to suffer physically.
And yet, in a mystical paradox of love, she requests the physical
suffering as well in order to be intimately united with Jesus Crucified, her suffering Son, in the most trying way imaginable.

That is love. It is selfless, genuine, and willing to endure anything for the Beloved.

That is the love of our holy Mother for Jesus! She loved Him
so tenderly that she would prefer to physically suffer the horrors
that He experienced—the merciless blows, the sharp thorns
penetrating the head, the piercing nails stabbing the flesh, the
horrifying scourging of the body—rather than see Him suffer all
alone. The Apostles, two of whom earlier in the Gospel requested
to be seated on His right and left when Jesus is in His glory—
the irony of the request is that, unbeknownst to them, it meant
being crucified with Him on His right and left—ran away out of
fear when the time of trial came rather than enduring the pains
that Jesus had to endure. His Mother, on the other hand, not only
stayed to offer a drop of comfort with her presence in the midst
of a sea of hatred and betrayal but also asked for the divine grace
that her Son would not have to suffer alone; that she too could
suffer everything with Him.

This is a remarkable reality that speaks of her person, of who
Mother Mary is. One cannot understand her without understanding this part of her personality and heart. Because in this
fact—in the fact that it would have been more painful for her to
see Jesus suffer alone than to request the grace of suffering with
Him (a grace that included unsurpassable torments of her body,
mind, and soul)—lies the pinnacle of her maternal love. The
depths of her Immaculate Heart—in its selflessness, sacrificial

nature, humility, and purity of intention; in its courageous and crucified love; in its single-minded devotion to God and the love of her Son—are all expressed here.

As Maria of Ágreda writes of the scourging of the Lord: "The divine blood flowed to the ground, gathering here and there in great abundance. The scourging in the face, and in the hands and feet, was unspeakably painful, because these parts are so full of sensitive and delicate nerves."[11] She continued to describe, in this context, Our Lady's participation in the suffering:

> I have already mentioned in other places of this history, and especially in that of the Passion, that the blessed Mother felt in her own body the torments of her Son. This was true also of the scourging, which She felt in all the parts of her virginal body, in the same intensity as they were felt by Christ in his body. Although She shed no blood except what flowed from her eyes with her tears, nor was lacerated in her flesh; yet the bodily pains so changed and disfigured Her, that saint John and the holy women failed to find in Her any resemblance of Herself.[12]

The Insights of Private Revelations

Private revelations of mystics do not, of course, have the same weight of authority as public revelation, the deposit of faith as revealed through Scripture and Tradition and as interpreted by the Magisterium as the official teaching body of the Church, that is, the pope and the bishops in union with him. What that also means is that private revelations of mystics are not perceived by the Church as *sources* for revelation because, again, those sources will come primarily from the two wings of public revelation,

---

[11] Maria of Ágreda, *Mystical City*, 537.
[12] Maria of Ágreda, *Mystical City*, 538.

Scripture and Tradition. However, private revelations can still offer *insights* of truth and even additional confirmations supporting the sources of revelation.

For example, when Pope Pius IX solemnly declared in 1854 the dogma of the Immaculate Conception, that dogmatic proclamation received considerable confirmation four years later when Our Lady appeared in the village of Lourdes, France, to the peasant girl Bernadette Soubirous and declared during her final apparition, "I am the Immaculate Conception."

Similarly, decades earlier in the 1830s, when another French visionary, this time Sister Catherine Labouré, received Marian apparitions, she was given a prayer that Mother Mary requested to be publicly promulgated on a devotional medal. This was the prayer on what would eventually become the famous Miraculous Medal: "O Mary, conceived without sin, pray for us who have recourse to thee." In the very language "conceived without sin" there was another insight into Our Lady's nature and the reality of the dogma of the Immaculate Conception.

Just like the Marian apparitions of Lourdes and of St. Catherine Labouré, the revelations that Maria of Ágreda received of Our Lady's life similarly presented strong support for the Immaculate Conception in the form of theological and historical narratives, offering further insights into the authenticity of the dogma. This does not mean that the revelations of these Marian visionaries were used as *sources* for the dogma, but it does mean that they helped offer additional, heavenly inspiration and confirmation, as approved apparitions (and, therefore, being "worthy of belief") to support the dogma.

What is also important to acknowledge in this case is that private revelations can, at times, *explicitly* articulate (and therefore support) what is only *implicitly* articulated in public revelation. That is to say, a truth may be present in rudimentary form in, say, the Bible, being contained therein *implicitly*, while the heavenly inspiration of an authentic private revelation may offer a more fully articulated definition of that truth.

We see this again in relation to the Immaculate Conception. Technically, the words "immaculate conception" do not appear anywhere in the Bible, thus the dogma is not *explicitly* pronounced in the Scriptures. However, it is certainly present implicitly. This is evident in sections like the Annunciation narrative in the Gospel of Luke. When the angel Gabriel greets Mary, he does so with the expressive salutation "Hail, full of grace" (Luke 1:28). Through his greeting, the heavenly messenger is telling us something about Mary's nature, about the state of her soul: that it is full of grace. This clearly implies that she was immaculately conceived and never touched by sin, as to be touched by sin would suggest being deprived of grace, of which she possessed a fullness in her soul.

Adam and Eve, in their state of original innocence, before the fall, would possess a fullness of grace that gave them a sublime communion with God. It was through sin that they (and the human race) lost that fullness of grace, that special union and relationship with God. Our Lady's Immaculate Conception constitutes a spiritual state of the soul that resembles that original state of innocence of our first parents. There is also a theological connection here between Eve and Mary.

The early Church Fathers famously identified Mary as the "New Eve," alongside Christ the Redeemer as the "New Adam." St. Jerome, masterfully summarizing the patristic view, expressed that death came through Eve, but life through Mary.[13]

Eve, through the temptation of a fallen angel, brought sin into the world. Mary, through the invitation of a holy angel, brought the source of salvation into the world, Jesus Christ. Eve, through the forbidden fruit of the tree of the knowledge of good

---

[13] St. Jerome, Epistle 22, "To Eustochium," in *A Select Library of Nicene and Post-Nicene Fathers of the Christian Church*, 2nd series, vol. 6, ed. Philip Schaff (Buffalo, NY: Christian Literature Publishing Co., 1893), https://www.newadvent.org/fathers/3001022.htm.

and evil, brought destruction and chaos into the world. Mary, through the "fruit of her womb" who died on the tree of life, the Cross, brought grace and restored order into the world. Eve, a pure virgin, fell through her disobedience; Mary, a pure virgin, was elevated by grace through her perfect obedience, a perfect obedience that culminated in the selfless and bloody sacrifice on Calvary of her beloved child, who ushered in the redemption of the world. Eve was symbolically called "mother of all living" (Gen 3:20); Mary became the Spiritual Mother of all the living, of the human race, and in a special way of those who are baptized (thus spiritually alive in their restoration to sonship with God).

To call her "full of grace," as the angel Gabriel does, is to connect Mary to the only other woman in history who was created without the stain of sin, in original innocence: Eve. No other person, man or woman, has come along in the history of time, since the original parents, who could be considered "full of grace" until Mary was conceived and born, a radiant light entering the darkness of a sinful world.

In the dynamic between implicitly present biblical truths that are often explicitly supported by other sources, we may have further support for the potential reality of Mary's stigmata. Let us consider this by turning to the Word of God and looking at an implicit truth that the Bible may hold about the interior wounds of the Mother of God.

A Source for Mary's Stigmata in the Bible

There may very well be a clear biblical reference supporting the interpretation of the mystical tradition that Our Lady possessed invisible stigmata, sharing intimately in the Crucifixion wounds of Jesus during His Passion. It is Simeon's prophecy in the Gospel of Luke, wherein filled with the Spirit the elder Simeon prophesies that the Child Jesus will be a "sign that is spoken against" and who will be responsible for the rise and fall of many in Israel and then turns to Our Lady and prophetically proclaims, "A sword will pierce through your own soul also" (Luke 2:34–35). Certain translations read "soul" while others read "heart"—either way, the reference is made to the core, or innermost part, of Mary's presence; as the heart, in biblical usage, symbolizes the interior depths of someone's personhood, or, one could say, their interior spirit or soul: who they are on the deepest level.

What theologians, especially Mariologists, generally agree upon is that the reference in Simeon's prophecy to the sword that shall pierce her is a reference to Our Lady's sufferings at the Passion and death of her Son. In other words, it is undoubtedly pointing toward the unspeakable pain and hurt that her heart must endure on the road to Calvary, her interior holocaust experiencing its culmination at the merciless Crucifixion and death of her child.

Let us also consider an interpretation of how the sword of Simeon prophecy can represent an interior piercing that not only speaks of an emotional and spiritual trauma of the highest degree but also can include interior stigmata, thus the "piercing" of physically felt pain that reveals a spiritually sublime union with Jesus, especially in the unique participation in His Passion. The symbolism of Catholic spirituality as well as fundamental theological principles support this interpretation of Simeon's prophecy. Let us begin with symbolism.

Symbolism of the Immaculate Heart

Essentially, what is being "pierced" in the biblical prophecy is Our Lady's Immaculate Heart. The Immaculate Heart is often depicted alongside the Sacred Heart of Jesus in both Catholic art and devotionals. One of those popular devotionals is, as referenced previously, the Miraculous Medal, the medal that St. Catherine Labouré received as a revelation from Our Lady during her Marian apparitions in the 1830s. Our Lady specifically provided an evolving apparition to St. Catherine that appeared in the pattern that the Miraculous Medal was to take. The front of the medal, as the apparition illustrated, included an image of Our Lady standing on a globe and from her hands exuding rays of light, which symbolized the graces that she mediates from heaven. An oval frame appeared around the apparition of Our Lady and within that frame a prayer materialized: "O Mary, conceived without sin, pray for us who have recourse to thee." It was a direct heavenly reference to the dogma of the Immaculate Conception, conferring Our Lady's identity as being purely conceived and thus preserved from all stain of sin from the earliest moment of her existence.

"Then," author Catherine M. Odell explains, "the frame reversed and the other side of the medal appeared."[14]

The other side contained a large M, which, as St. Catherine Labouré wrote, was "surmounted by a cross, having a double bar under it. Beneath this M, the holy hearts of Jesus and Mary were placed, side by side, the first crowned with thorns, the other pierced by a sword. Around the whole were twelve stars."[15]

It is interesting how, at times, a popular devotional—particularly one like the Miraculous Medal, which has reached millions, if not billions, of Catholics worldwide—can hold within it deep theological truths. The Miraculous Medal provides a catechesis of Mariology in its rich symbolism and illustrious spirituality. While the front of the medal clearly reveals such truths as Our Lady's identity as advocate, mediatrix of graces, and the Immaculate Conception, the back of the medal especially emphasizes the unique participation that Our Lady had with the suffering of Jesus during His Passion. It is seen both in the large M that is surmounted by the Cross, and with the placement of the

---

[14] Catherine M. Odell, *Those Who Saw Her: Apparitions of Mary* (Huntington, IN: Our Sunday Visitor, 2010), 73.

[15] Odell, *Those Who Saw Her*, 73.

holy hearts of Jesus and Mary alongside each other, the former crowned with thorns, the latter pierced by a sword.

The image of the Sacred Heart of Jesus, crowned with thorns, does pertain to a *physical* (and thus bodily) suffering that He endured, but it is also multifarious and multidimensional in its symbolism, signifying numerous aspects of the Lord's Passion, particularly through the core image of the heart—constituting all that the poor Jesus had to endure in the trauma that He selflessly embraced for us. On a literal level, it is the crown of thorns that we see. On a symbolic level, it is His heart that is crowned with thorns, representing a totality of suffering that His entire being had to experience: physical, emotional, and spiritual.

Physically, the crown of thorns unmercifully pierced the sensitive and already suffering head of Jesus, its sharp and penetrating thorns producing unbearable pain. Emotionally, the crown of thorns produced humiliation and mockery toward Jesus's humanity, profound insult being added to physical injury by a cruel and heartless mockery of Jesus's identity, meant to embarrass and deeply hurt Him. Spiritually, the crown of thorns was a blasphemy, men (and the demons who inspired them) attempting to mock the royalty dignity of God.

I, therefore, suggest that the image of the Immaculate Heart of Mary being pierced by a sword also corresponds—as the New Eve so often does to the New Adam—to the threefold torture of Jesus, which was physical, emotional, and spiritual in its totality.

Physically, this would include Our Lady suffering interior stigmata, physically experiencing and feeling within her own body the excruciating pains that her Son, Jesus, endured. Emotionally, this would include her broken heart as a mother, experiencing an inconsolable anguish at seeing how cruelly men have treated and abused her innocent child, to the point of unmercifully torturing and killing Him. Spiritually, this would include Our Lady's interior experience of the dark night and her special, supernatural insight into the divine reality of who Jesus is as God and the mission that He was accomplishing, understanding like no one else the horrible blasphemy that was committed against the divine majesty. On this final, spiritual level it is important to remember that Our Lady, according to the *Mystical City of God*, asked for the grace not only to share in the physical sufferings of her Son but also to have all consolation taken away from her so that He would not have to suffer the spiritual anguish of the interior darkness by Himself, alone.

Therefore, it is quite possible that when Simeon prophesied that a sword shall pierce Our Lady's soul, that "piercing" existed on every level—physical, emotional, and spiritual—corresponding to the way that Jesus suffered in His totality. This reality of the special participation in Christ's wounds is also strongly rooted in theology, specifically important theological and spiritual principles that are essential to understanding the Blessed Virgin Mary. Let us turn our attention there.

The Principle of Preeminence and the Wound of Love

Because Our Lady was immaculately conceived, thus preserved from original sin and its effects, she would possess a fullness of grace. Hence, the angel can greet and identify her with the words "Hail, full of grace" (Luke 1:28) as a greeting that pertains to her identity. That fullness of grace means that Our Lady lived in a state of sanctifying grace and that she had the fullness of virtues and graces that we receive from our baptism, except in a much greater measure, transcending that of all the saints. Theologically, this is known as the "principle of preeminence."

Expounding on the principle, Fr. James Brent, O.P., explains, "Mary was preeminent among the saints. What does that mean specifically? She received, in the fullest measure, all the supernatural favors and graces accorded to the other saints. So, whatever the other saints had Mary had in a higher way."[16] Fr. Brent articulates what this would look like through a helpful comparison with one of the greatest mystics of the Dominican order: "Here's one way to maybe make it a little more concrete: think of the most mystical saints you can, think perhaps of St. Catherine of Siena. Whatever there was in St. Catherine of Siena and her personal familiarity with God, the Blessed Virgin Mary had that, but in a manner greater than Catherine of Siena."[17] One extraordinary grace that Catherine of Siena possessed, which signified her personal familiarity and deep union with God through the form of Jesus Crucified, was invisible stigmata. The Blessed Virgin Mary would, therefore, possess that grace of invisible stigmata but in greater measure—corresponding, according to Maria of Ágreda and other mystics, to every pain during the Passion that Jesus was enduring.

Catherine's invisible stigmata included feeling the pains of Christ's wounds on her hands and feet, and also in an interior way on her heart. This is a phenomenon that can also be called a "wound of love," a type of deep interior pain and yearning (especially felt in the heart) for union with Jesus Crucified that a person who is ascending in the spiritual life and reaching greater depths of mystical intimacy may experience.[18] Here we especially have the

---

[16] The Thomistic Institute, "The Contemplative Life of the Blessed Virgin Mary," YouTube video, 58:13, May 13, 2021, https://www.youtube.com/watch?v=aRaijDYqL-Q.

[17] Fr. Brent continues, "Or think of all the mystical graces and contemplative life that St. Teresa of Avila had. The Blessed Virgin Mary was greater than Teresa of Avila, or John of the Cross, or Therese of Lisieux, or St. Elizabeth of the Trinity, or whatever other saint you might name who has lived a deep union with God in prayer; the Blessed Virgin Mary was greater. She was the ultimate contemplative soul, after Jesus Christ himself, of course." "The Contemplative Life of the Blessed Virgin Mary."

[18] Fr. Marin writes about experiences that are present when a soul has entered the highest, unitive grades of prayer—meaning, in the unitive state of the spiritual life. Among the phenomena experienced, he writes of what St. John of the Cross and St. Teresa of Avila depicted in their works as the "fiery darts of

stigmatic connection to Simeon's prophecy about the sword piercing Mother Mary's heart, and there is an allusion in the Song of Songs which has been interpreted as the interior reality of such a wound, "I am wounded with love" (see Song 2:5).

As a spiritual director, I have had the opportunity to encounter a number of humble and holy souls who have had profound mystical experiences of God's unitive love, among them a couple of contemporary stigmatics—a phenomenon that is much more common in its interior, invisible manifestation. One former directee of mine was a young woman who, during certain intimate moments of prayer, would tangibly feel the wounds of Christ in her hands and feet, and also on her heart. It was the wound on the heart that seemed most painful to her because in addition to physical pain—a type of physical burning sensation that she felt—the wound possessed an intense, at times overpowering, spiritual and emotional yearning for Jesus—hence, a "wound of love"—that carried its own mystical combination of joy and pain.

Talk about a pierced heart!

Another reason as to why the wound on the heart was more painful is because it was the one that was constant—meaning, even if the other wounds on the hands and feet were not felt, the one on the heart remained. It also predated the others, being

---

love" and a successive experience known as "wounds of love." Regarding the "fiery darts of love," Fr. Marin explains, "St. Teresa of Avila describes this phenomenon as a wounding of the soul, as if an arrow had pierced the soul. It causes the soul great affliction, and at the same time is very delectable. The wound is not a physical one, but it is deep within the soul and seems to spring from the soul's inmost depths. It arouses profound desires for God and a kind of hatred of the body." The hatred of the body comes not in an unhealthy way but due to the soul's fiercely amorous desire to be fully united with God, the body being perceived as a remaining obstacle that keeps the soul from that ecstatic union. The "wounds of love," Fr. Marin explains, "are similar to the preceding phenomenon, but they are more profound and more lasting. . . . The soul lovingly complains to God at not being able to leave this life and to enjoy the intimate union with him in heaven." See Marin, *Theology of Christian Perfection*, 550.

the original wound from which the others emanated, it could be said. It is an honor for a spiritual director to encounter in a humble, holy soul who is trying to understand her experiences a lived expression of the mystical life that great saints and mystics have written of. People experience profound graces of unitive love with the living and resurrected Christ. These graces are seen both in ages past, from the lives of great medieval mystics and saints like Catherine of Siena, and in our current times in contemporary human beings, the hidden mystics among us, who have intensely intimate spiritual lives.

St. John of the Cross, the Mystical Doctor, wrote about the interior wound of love in the second stanza of *The Living Flame of Love*. What is significant, especially if we consider the possibility that this mystical interior wound is referenced in Simeon's prophecy about Our Lady's pierced heart, is that John specifically connects the wound of love to manifestations of the stigmata. "God usually does not bestow a favor on the body without bestowing it first and principally on the soul," St. John writes. "Thus the greater the delight and strength of love the wound produces in the soul, so much greater is that produced by the wound outside on the body, and when there is an increase in one there is an increase in the other."[19] Thus, the character of the exterior manifestation of stigmata will be proportional to the character of the interior wound of love.

This is the manner in which St. John understands and analyzes St. Francis's experience of the stigmata. He writes of the cruciform seraph whom Francis experienced when he received the sacred wounds:

---

[19] St. John on the Cross, *The Living Flame of Love*, in *The Collected Works of St. John of the Cross*, trans. Kieran Kavanaugh, O.C.D., and Otilio Rodriguez, O.C.D. (Washington, DC: Institute of Carmelite Studies, 1997), 662.

Let us return to the work of that seraph, for he truly inflicts a sore, and wounds inwardly in the spirit. Thus, if God sometimes permits an effect to extend to the bodily senses in the fashion in which it existed interiorly, the wound and sore appear outwardly, as happened when the seraph wounded St. Francis. When his soul was wounded with love by the five wounds, their effect extended to the body, and these wounds were impressed on the body, which was wounded just as his soul was wounded with love.[20]

Notice how John articulates that it was first the soul which "was wounded with love by the five wounds," and *thereafter* the effect of this spiritual wounding extended to the body. Meaning, the stigmata began with an interior wounding, emanating from the inner life, which experiences a deep, transforming union with Christ that leads to an exterior manifestation of that union in the body, the person becoming a living icon of Christ through an intimate sharing of His Passion in the flesh.

It begins from within. In this case, the stigmata resembles an interior piercing of love that is so intense that the soul cannot hold it back, and it emanates from within into the parts of the body: the Crucified Christ emanating from within the person with His piercing love. St. John writes that "an effect of the spirit overflows into the senses. When this is true, the effect in the senses proceeds from an abundance of spirit, as in the event of the wounds that proceed from the inner strength and appear outwardly. This happened to St. Paul, whose immense compassion for the sufferings of Christ redounded in the body, as he explains to the Galatians: I bear the wounds of the Lord Jesus in my body [Gal. 6:17]."[21]

St. John of the Cross interprets St. Paul's words to the

---

[20] John of the Cross, *The Living Flame of Love*, 662.
[21] John of the Cross, *The Living Flame of Love*, 663.

Galatians as a reference to stigmata wounds. There are debates among theologians and biblical scholars whether Paul was actually making reference to stigmata here. Whether or not he was is not of concern for our purposes. What concerns us is the understanding of stigmata that John of the Cross had as a Doctor of the Church, as the Mystical Doctor who held a profound grasp of mystical theology. Consider the aspects of John's understanding of stigmata that would strongly support the argument that Mother Mary possessed interior stigmata wounds.

First, it is an interior wound of love for Jesus that the soul possesses, the soul being pierced with this wound, which can overflow into the senses and emanate in stigmata wounds. Second, the possibility of the exterior wounds is proportional to the intensity of the piercing love that is present within the soul through the inner wound. "Thus the greater the delight and strength of love the wound produces in the soul, so much greater is that produced by the wound outside on the body, and when there is an increase in the one there is an increase in the other. This so happens because these souls are purified and established in God."[22] Notice here how John connects the degree of purification that a soul has received with the intensity of the wounds, interior and exterior, that are experienced.

In all these measures, it would make theological sense for Our Lady to have an experience of the stigmata. Her soul was pierced like no other—there was no heart that had as deep and intimate of a spiritual union with the Sacred Heart of Jesus as the Immaculate Heart of Mary, the New Eve with the New Adam. Flesh of her flesh, who had to be born of an immaculate woman to receive her immaculate human nature. There was no soul that was as pure as her own, she who was full of grace. Thus, if there is a correspondence to the intensity of those wounds of love with the degree of purification that a soul has experienced, then in Our

---

[22] John of the Cross, *The Living Flame of Love*, 662.

Lady we have a soul who was completely pure and would, there-fore, experience the greatest intensity of wounded love for Christ. It is fitting, therefore, that the interior depths of her spiritual union with her Son would overflow to an experience of the body, feeling His pain intimately in her flesh, a pain that originates from the innermost transpiercing communion of Hearts that Jesus and Mary would mystically share. Hence, Simeon can say, "A sword will pierce through your own soul also" (Luke 2:35).

An objection may be voiced, articulating that Simeon's proph-ecy is a clear reference to the pain of unfathomable grief that Mother Mary would experience at Calvary and not to a mysti-cal wound of love that leads to interior stigmata. The response to this objection is simple: the holy Scriptures have such a depth of gravity and meaning that is multidimensional that significant pas-sages can have multilayered readings. A single passage can possess within itself a historical, allegorical (or spiritual), anagogical, and topographical (or moral) interpretation—in other words, all of the above. The fact that it is a passage pertaining to prophecy further accentuates this point, as prophetic utterances are famously multilayered in their meanings.[23] Thus, Simeon's prophecy, in its multifarious richness, speaks to the historical significance of Mother Mary's grief at Calvary and can simultaneously speak to the mystical depths of her wound of love, spiritually overflowing to the point of an interior sharing in Christ's pain through inner stigmata during His Passion. Yes, Simeon's prophecy is a refer-ence to Calvary—but, potentially, in more ways than one.

On a spiritual and theological level, since she was full of grace, no one would have as strong of a communion with Jesus—no matter how great the mystic or saint—as Mother Mary. She would experience, as the principle of predominance theologically

---

[23] See the masterful work of Niels Christian Hvidt on this topic: *Christian Prophecy: The Post-Biblical Tradition* (New York: Oxford University Press, 2007).

explains, a greater measure of graces, including mystical graces, than any other saint who ever lived. Hence, it makes theo*logical* sense, and is in fact fitting, to believe in her interior and invisible stigmata as a particularly special communion of crucified love with Him who was her own flesh, Jesus. She gave Him His flesh, and interiorly shared in the wounds of that flesh.

What the holy Scriptures implicitly tell us through Simeon's prophecy, and the revelations of mystics like the Venerable Maria of Ágreda explicitly reveal, and what devotions like the Miraculous Medal support in their symbolism, Catholic theology itself vindicates through the principle of preeminence and supports through the mystical theology of Church Doctors like St. John of the Cross and St. Teresa of Avila (who also wrote of "wounds of love"). Mother Mary, very likely, was the first stigmatic, experiencing the interior wounds of Christ as He was undergoing the horrific and life-giving ordeal that was the Passion. If certain saints have had this unitive experience of crucified love with Christ, then the Virgin Mary had it in the greatest measure.

However, what makes her interior stigmata most impressive is not the supernatural grace itself of the felt pain and interior anguish but the fact that, according to the *Mystical City of God*, Our Lady asked God for the grace of suffering in this excruciating way with her beloved Jesus, so that He may not have to suffer alone. In this selfless act of heart-wrenching intimacy lies the secret to understanding the person and the beauty of our most kindhearted, sorrowful Mother, of who she is in her tender love.

Chapter 6

Hearing Her Voice, Consoling Her Heart

Listen and be sure, my dear son, that I will protect you; do not be
frightened or grieved or let your heart be dismayed. . . . Am I not here, I
who am your Mother, and is not my help a refuge?
　　　　　　　　　　　　　　—*Our Lady to St. Juan Diego, 1531*

My daughter, look at my Heart encircled with the thorns [with] which
ungrateful men pierce it at every moment by their blasphemies and
ingratitude.
　　　　　　　　　　—*Our Lady to Sister Lucia dos Santos, 1925*

Often, I am asked by one of my students, "How do I grow in
Marian devotion, in my love of Mary?"

"One of the essential things necessary to grow in love of her," I
respond, "is to be able to hear her voice. And in order to hear her
voice, you need to read about her apparitions."

Strong Marian devotees understand this reality well. They
follow her apparitions. They know her voice. They understand
that tender, maternal caress that stirs the soul through her warm
and loving words.

Consider, for example, how tenderly Our Lady of Guadalupe
spoke to Juan Diego during her famous apparitions of 1531. The
very name by which she called Juan speaks volumes to her sincere
love and gentleness toward him as his Spiritual Mother.

"Juanito, my sweet child, where are you going?"

Catherine Odell writes of this first encounter, "A young woman, strikingly beautiful, stood there, beckoning him. She radiated such light and joy that Juan Diego could think of nothing more to do than drop to his knees and smile at her."[1]

When she addressed him as "Juanito," an affectionate name meaning "Little John," and referred to him "as my sweet child," she did so in Nahuatl, Juan Diego's native tongue.[2]

The loving name of endearment, the decision to speak in his native language, the address of a consoling mother to her "sweet child," all signify who she is. Her voice reveals her personality and presence, as a mother of the deepest warmth and caring concern for her children. She would go on to tell Juan Diego:

> I am your merciful Mother, the Mother of all of you who live united in this land, and of all mankind, of all those who love me, of those who cry to me, of those who seek me, of those who have confidence in me. Here I will hear their weeping, their sorrow, and will remedy and alleviate their suffering, necessities, and misfortunes.[3]

We see in this message a sweet mother who not only wants to hear the weeping and sorrow of her children but also deeply desires to remedy their suffering, needs, and misfortunes. Juan Diego experienced this side of Our Lady very personally. He believed himself to be unworthy of the mission that she was bestowing upon him, as she sent him to go to the bishop's house to request that a sanctuary be built on the spot of her apparitions. Furthermore, Juan had an uncle who was terribly ill and believed that the responsibility of caring for him was further reason why he was not the right person for the mission.

---

[1] Catherine M. Odell, *Those Who Saw Her: Apparitions of Mary* (Huntington, IN: Our Sunday Visitor, 2010), 40.

[2] Odell, *Those Who Saw Her*, 40.

[3] Odell, *Those Who Saw Her*, 41.

"What troubles you, my dear son?" the Virgin Mary asked him, as Juan tried to avoid meeting her another time, given all his insecurities. "Where are you going?" she inquired.[4]

When Juan shared his concerns about his ill uncle, and how there was no one else to care for him, and why the mission that she gave him was being delayed, the Blessed Mother replied with the most affectionate understanding and reassurance toward him:

> Listen and be sure, my dear son, that I will protect you; do not be frightened or grieved or let your heart be dismayed, however great the illness may be that you speak of. Am I not here, I who am your Mother, and is not my help a refuge? Am I not of your kind? Do not be concerned about your uncle's illness, for he is not going to die. Be assured, he is already well. Is there anything else that you need?[5]

Hearing Our Lady's messages, and thus spiritually internalizing her voice for the consolation of the soul, is important for a couple of reasons. One is, as mentioned above, to receive a better sense of who she is, of her personality and her loving, maternal presence. The beauty of an authentic Marian apparition is that there is a felt presence. Even if a person is not chosen to be a visionary (as most people are not), that person can still read about, study, or watch films and documentaries about a given Marian apparition in order to better comprehend the spiritual presence of the Mother who encourages, admonishes, supports, and prays for her children.

One does not need to be St. Bernadette in order to read about the apparitions of Lourdes or to watch a beautiful film like *The Song of Bernadette* and feel within the interior regions of one's soul the spiritual aching and longing for a sacred encounter with the

---

4   Odell, *Those Who Saw Her*, 44.
5   Odell, *Those Who Saw Her*, 44.

sweet, maternal presence that speaks to the visionary. That sacred encounter, of course, will not be of the same nature as the visionary is experiencing; it will not be a supernatural apparition, but it will be something holy and special, an interior movement of grace that is touching the soul, melting the heart, and inspiring the person toward a conversion of life. The person feels, perhaps more so than ever before, that Jesus is real, that the Eucharist is real, that the Catholic faith is true, vibrant, and life-giving because the Mother of Christ is helping awaken a part of the soul that has been dormant or asleep for too long with her loving, healing voice that (unlike countless sermons or theological talks) is actually inspiring interior transformation through a supernatural flood of grace, a holy warmth that represents the caress of the Holy Spirit.

A second reason as to why it is important to listen to Our Lady's messages and hear her voice is to help aid her co-redemptive mission with Jesus. That is to say, Mother Mary, on behalf of God, wants to inspire her children to live lives of deep meaning, and there is no greater meaning than to give one's life to Jesus Christ for the salvation of souls, for the advancement and glory of the Kingdom of God. To "give one's life to Jesus Christ for the salvation of souls" does not mean that every person needs to become a priest or religious sister; no, for not everyone is called to such a vocation. What it does mean is that every person is called within their individual vocations to be a man or woman of prayer, sacrifice, and holy charity, a living light, an instrument that Jesus and Mary can use to bring others to them, to work for the betterment of being and the salvation of souls.

An overview of every major Marian apparition would be beyond the scope of this writing. However, we will give attention in the following pages to the great apparitions of Fatima, one of the most important Marian events of the twentieth century, and arguably of any century. For in Fatima, not only did Our Lady appear, not only did the sun dance in the sky in a miraculous manner, showing nearly seventy thousand people that the supernatural is real, but she also gave a message of deep substance and urgency which speaks to the importance of life, the eternal consequences of our actions, and the significant role that each one of us has to play in the battle between heaven and hell.

Our Lady's Message

It is an interesting, but little-known, fact that the great Marian apparitions of Fatima, which transpired in 1917, were actually prefigured by a set of angelic apparitions, which began in 1916. The first time that the angel appeared to the three shepherd children, Lucia dos Santos and siblings Francisco and Jacinta Marto, he said, "Do not be afraid! I am the Angel of Peace. Pray with me."[6]

According to the children, the angel knelt down and touched his forehead to the ground, asking them to repeat a prayer with him three times: "My God, I believe, I adore, I trust, and I love You. I ask pardon for those who do not believe, do not adore, do not trust, and do not love You."[7]

This simple prayer, rich in theological significance, was preparation for the children to adopt a spirituality of reparation, which subsequent messages, both angelic and those from Our Lady, would make more apparent.

In the summer of 1916, finding the children playing in a family garden, the angel returned a second time and said to them, "What are you doing? Pray! Pray much! The Hearts of Jesus and Mary have designs upon you. Offer prayers and sacrifices constantly to the Most High."[8]

The angelic message here is reminiscent of and resembles highly the message that St. Michael the Archangel gave to a young

---

[6] Jean M. Heimann, *Fatima: The Apparition That Changed the World* (Charlotte, NC: TAN Books, 2017), 1.

[7] Heimann, *Fatima*, 1.

[8] Heimann, *Fatima*, 2.

Joan of Arc centuries earlier, when Joan, playing in her parents' garden, experienced after a strong glare of light the audible voice of St. Michael speaking to her with the words, "Be a good girl, Joan, and pious. Great things are expected of you."[9]

Here even the young ones, children, are told that there is a great design on their lives, that heaven has big expectations of them to live lives of depth and meaning, which begins with cultivating a strong interior life of the Spirit.

During this second apparition, Lucia asked the angel, "How must we sacrifice?"

The angel replied, "Make of everything you can a sacrifice and offer it to God as an act of reparation for the sins by which He is offended and in supplication for the conversion of sinners. You will thus draw down peace upon your country. I am its Guardian Angel, the Angel of Portugal. Above all, accept and bear with submission the suffering which the Lord will send you."[10]

In this message there is a teaching—numerous teachings, in fact. A central one is that daily sacrifices can take form in two ways: actively or passively. Active sacrifices are the voluntary renunciations that we choose, such as fasting on bread and water or giving up meat or sweets or technology, and actively offer to God as an act of reparation and for the conversion of sinners. The angelic message also stresses passive sacrifices. This pertains to bearing with humble submission and acceptance the sufferings that the Lord allows in our lives, which can also be offered up as an act of reparation or for the conversion of sinners.

Let us continue on to the third message before we unpack more of the richness of the spirituality here.

A major reason as to why the third apparition is highly important is the Eucharistic significance. Even before the angel

---

9 Jay Williams, *Joan of Arc: Warrior Saint* (New York/London: Sterling Publishing, 2007), 5.
10 Heimann, *Fatima*, 2.

said anything, his actions were filled with deeply sublime meaning. As he held a golden chalice in his hand, with the Eucharistic Host above it, red drops of the Precious Blood fell into the chalice from the Host. While the Host was suspended in midair, the angel bowed with great reverence. As he pressed his forehead to the ground, the angel asked the children to, three times, repeat the following prayer:

> O Most Holy Trinity—Father, Son and Holy Spirit—I adore Thee profoundly. I offer Thee the most precious Body, Blood, Soul and Divinity of Jesus Christ, present in all the tabernacles of the world, in reparation for the outrages, sacrileges, and indifferences whereby He is offended. And through the infinite merits of His Most Sacred Heart and the Immaculate Heart of Mary, I beg of Thee the conversion of poor sinners.[11]

Then the angel offered the Host to Lucia and the Precious Blood to Francisco and Jacinta, telling the children to take "and drink the Body and Blood of Jesus Christ, horribly outraged by ungrateful men! Make reparation for their crimes and console your God!"[12]

We live in a time wherein there is very little belief in, or reverence for, the Eucharist, or for the existence of angels, for that matter. A popular Pew survey that came out in 2019 documented the travesty that nearly 70 percent of Catholics do not believe in the Real Presence of Jesus Christ in the Eucharist.[13] That is an absolute tragedy of faith since the Eucharist is at the center of

---

[11] Heimann, *Fatima*, 2.

[12] Heimann, *Fatima*, 3.

[13] Gregory A. Smith, "Just One-third of U.S. Catholics Agree with Their Church That Eucharist Is Body, Blood of Christ," *Pew Research Center*, August 5, 2019, https://www.pewresearch.org/fact-tank/2019/08/05/transubstantiation-eucharist-u-s-catholics/.

Catholicism, the source and summit; to deny it is as paramount as denying the Incarnation and Resurrection of Jesus Christ.

In light of these troubling realities, the apparitions of Fatima, including the angelic apparitions that predate Our Lady's appearances, take on even greater value, for they remind us of forgotten sacred truths. And it is important in life to come back to forgotten sacred truths because they lead us to meaningful, moral, and spiritually fulfilling lives that affect us and those around us deeply, and that have eternal ramifications for our souls. "Stand by the roads, and look, and ask for the ancient paths, where the good way is; and walk in it, and find rest for your souls" (Jer 6:16).

The third message of the angel, a short but exquisite prayer in its profundity, makes clear in front of the Holy Trinity that the real presence of Jesus Christ in the Eucharist is the authentic truth, acknowledging that in His Body, Blood, Soul, and Divinity, He is present in the Eucharist, "in all the tabernacles of the world." The message also makes clear that one can make Communions of reparation—this is a spirituality that Our Lady will articulate in greater detail in the Fatima message—in "reparation for the outrages, sacrileges, and indifferences" by which God is offended. Here the reverent reception of the Eucharist can have a reparatory value, when offered up to God with the purpose of making reparation for sins of ingratitude and sacrileges.

The third part of the message possesses strong co-redemptive symbolism, as it pleads for the conversion of poor sinners "through the infinite merits of His Most Sacred Heart and the Immaculate Heart of Mary." In any authentic co-redemptive Mariology, it is never said that Mary is equal to Jesus in any way; it is simply said that she had the most singular and unique role (and continues to have unique cooperation) in helping Jesus save souls. This is not a controversial teaching at all, as no other person can say that they are the Immaculate Conception and the Mother of God, and as even magisterial documents of the Second Vatican Council, such as the Dogmatic Constitution on the Church *Lumen Gentium*, have acknowledged her singular and unique cooperation in helping Jesus redeem souls. "She conceived, brought forth and nourished Christ. She presented Him to the Father in the temple, and was united with Him by compassion as He died on the Cross. In this singular way she cooperated by her obedience, faith, hope and burning charity in the work of the Saviour in giving back supernatural life to souls. Wherefore she is our mother in the order of grace."[14]

After the angelic apparitions, Our Lady first appeared to the visionaries of Fatima on May 13, 1917. As an adult, Lucia described the luminous apparition of the Mother of God thus: "She was more brilliant than the sun, and radiated light more clear and intense than a crystal glass filled with sparkling water when the rays of the burning sun shine through it."[15]

Our Lady explained that she is from heaven, asked the visionaries to return for six successive months on the thirteenth day to receive her messages, and she also asked the children to pray the Rosary each day to obtain peace for the world and an end to the war, as her apparitions took place in the midst of the First World War. It was at Fatima that she identified herself under the title of Our Lady of the Rosary.[16]

Amongst the words that she spoke to them that first day, the following had great value, and in many ways repeated explicitly the message that the angel had been communicating: "Are you willing to offer yourselves to God and bear all the sufferings He wills to send you, as an act of reparation for the sins by which He is offended, and of supplication for the conversion of sinners?"[17]

When the children answered in the affirmative, that they were

---

[14] Second Vatican Council, Dogmatic Constitution on the Church *Lumen Gentium* (1964), §61.
[15] Heimann, *Fatima*, 11.
[16] Odell, *Those Who Saw Her*, 145.
[17] Heimann, *Fatima*, 12.

willing, Mother Mary responded, "Then you are going to have much to suffer, but the grace of God will be your comfort."[18]

It was during her third apparition, which took place on July 13 of that year, that Our Lady reinforced the message of reparation, stressing the need for sacrifices, and gave the visionaries a prayer to pray when offering such sacrifices. "Sacrifice yourselves for sinners and say many times, especially when you make a sacrifice: 'O Jesus, this is for love of Thee, for the conversion of sinners, and in reparation for the sins committed against the Immaculate Heart of Mary.'"[19] It was the first message that spoke specifically about making reparation to her Immaculate Heart. What followed would become one of the most influential and consequential experiences of the young visionaries' lives.

They were shown, as if it were happening right in front of them, a horrific vision of hell. The children described seeing a great sea of fire. Plunged into the sea of fire, the children saw demons and souls in human form, "amid shrieks and groans of pain and despair, which horrified us and made us tremble with fear. . . . The demons could be distinguished by their terrifying and repellent likeness to frightful and unknown animals, black and transparent like burning coals."[20] The children turned toward Our Lady, looking for consolation during the horrendous vision.

The Mother of God explained to them that they had been shown hell, the dreadful suffering that sin causes. Our Lady told them that in order to save sinners, God wanted to establish worldwide devotion to her Immaculate Heart, and she emphasized that if the visionaries did what she requested, many would be saved. Another one of her messages would stress the intercessory importance of prayers and penances as an instrumental way to help souls who are on the verge of hell. "Pray, pray very much,

---

[18] Heimann, *Fatima*, 12.

[19] Heimann, *Fatima*, 30.

[20] As quoted in Heimann, *Fatima*, 30.

and make sacrifices for sinners; for many souls go to hell, because there are none to sacrifice themselves and to pray for them."[21]

Interestingly, just a few years later, in His revelations to St. Faustina, Jesus gave a similar message, telling the apostle of Divine Mercy, "Pray as much as you can for the dying. By your entreaties obtain for them trust in My mercy, because they have most need of trust, and have it least. Be assured that the grace of eternal salvation for certain souls in their final moment depends on your prayer."[22]

These messages speak to an incredible, life-altering reality about the high importance of prayer in the life of intercession. The reality that a human being's eternal salvation, the fact that their soul can spend all eternity in heaven or hell, can be contingent on one's prayer speaks volumes to the responsibility that we Christians have in following the inspiration and grace of praying for others, especially the dying and those who are on the verge of hell.

At Lourdes, although briefer in communication, Our Lady's message was similar. Penitence, she told Bernadette, was what she expected and wanted from everyone. Furthermore, "Pray to God for the conversion of sinners."[23]

Notice that Our Lady comes from heaven with a mission of urgency to help save her children from persisting on the wrong path of life, from the path that leads to damnation, to the fires of hell. She is a caring mother who also invites us to cooperate in this work of co-redemption with her. She tells us that she needs our prayers and sacrifices for the fulfillment of this mission, this work of grace.

And that is one of the most striking realities, something to ponder upon and contemplate: the fact that the Mother of God

---

[21] Bishop Thomas J. Olmstead, "The Fatima Prayer," *The Catholic Sun*, August 16, 2017, https://www.catholicsun.org/2017/08/16/the-fatima-prayer/.

[22] St. Faustina Maria Kowalska, *Divine Mercy in My Soul: Diary of Saint Maria Faustina Kowalska* (Stockbridge, MA: Marian Press, 2011), no. 1777.

[23] Odell, *Those Who Saw Her*, 104.

needs me for the fulfillment of her mission, the important mission that her Son has entrusted to her. Who am I, a person may think, that the Mother of God, the Queen of Heaven and earth, needs me? Here we begin to see the absolute honor of this relationship. My life can play a role in helping the Mother of Jesus Christ to save souls from the grasp of demons and the fires of hell; it has eternal consequences that will forever be felt and affect human lives in the most urgent and significant way imaginable.

The messages of Fatima, beginning with the angelic apparitions and continuing into the Marian, highlight—as has been observed above—two major themes: the need to make reparation and the need to pray and sacrifice for the conversion of sinners. Living out these two messages that Our Lady invites us into gives life profound meaning. These two messages are also intrinsically connected. Let us observe each in detail, beginning with what exactly it means to make reparation and how can we do so best.

Making Reparation

There is a hauntingly beautiful scene in the 2020 film *Fatima*. The three shepherd children are experiencing an apparition of Mother Mary. Behind them, a large crowd is present. At one point, there is a moment of ingratitude expressed by a woman in the crowd. Our Lady looks at the visionaries with a deep, silent sadness. She slowly opens her veil and reveals interior thorns piercing her heart from within. Blood drips down her white dress, as she lowers her head in sadness.

"I'm sorry, Mother," Lucia says in heart-wrenching angst.[24]

Our Lady quietly shakes her head, tears welling up in her eyes.

The scene is incredibly powerful because what we are witnessing is a real woman experiencing pain and deep hurt. When we

---

[24] *Fatima*, directed by Marco Pontecorvo (NBC Universal/Picturehouse, 2020), https://www.youtube.com/watch?v=YFM7Ebqf7uU.

are used to seeing so many artistic and devotional portrayals of Our Lady, whether they are in the form of paintings, sculptures, or icons, it is often easy to feel a type of emotional distance, the artform not always being able to capture the humanity of the person. But that is the advantage that film as a genre has; through the portrayal of an actress, we see a real person, and we are vividly reminded that the Blessed Virgin Mary is a real human person who still suffers for us and whose suffering we can help alleviate through acts of reparation.

Making reparation is one of the most poignant and, conversely, least known and least understood, expressions of spirituality in Catholicism. To make reparation is to make amends for offenses and insults given to God and to the Mother of God through the sins of humanity, especially through blasphemies, sacrileges, and ingratitude. The ingratitude is intrinsically connected to the Passion, the reality that Jesus endured, out of love for each human person, unspeakable horrors of torture, of humiliation, of physical, emotional, and spiritual agony. And that sacred act of Love, which is the Passion, is ridiculed and mocked by so many souls throughout the world who couldn't care less about it, who make the daily decision to live lives engrossed in mortal sin, the sins which crucified Jesus, as if His sacrifice means nothing.

Reparation, therefore, has two main elements: consolation and co-redemption. Through an act of reparation, the human person is able to console Jesus and Mary, and that becomes a beautiful act of intimacy and love offered to their pierced Hearts. It is a profound privilege, the reality that a human creature can console God or the Mother of God. I love the example that my colleague from the theology department at Franciscan University of Steubenville, the Mariologist Mark Miravalle—whose work first introduced me to a better understanding and appreciation of this theology of reparation—gives in relation to consoling the Immaculate Heart of Mary. I have heard Dr. Miravalle articulate and provide in a lecture an analogy which beautifully illustrates both the heartfelt angst and affection behind a spirituality of reparation. He used the analogy of a child offending its mother, leaving her in tears, and then another child, the sibling, coming up to the sorrowful mother and lovingly embracing her in order to console her as she suffers emotionally from the offenses that the first child's behavior provided.

This is a beautiful and useful analogy, as it speaks to how we can console the tears of our Spiritual Mother, Mother Mary, especially due to the suffering that she must endure because of the sins of so many ungrateful children, whom she loves immensely, but who—unfortunately—do not return that love. It is a tragedy when Love is not loved, a tragedy that both Jesus Crucified and our sorrowful Mother have to experience too frequently because of their children.

When we console Our Lady's Heart through acts of reparation, we are saying to her, "Mom, I'm so sorry that you've had to experience this offense. I'm so sorry that there are those who are ungrateful to you, and to Jesus for the gift of His Passion. But please know that I am here, and I love you. And I am sorry for any time that my life or decisions have not reflected that love. I am here to wipe the tears from your eyes. Please receive my love."

It is, in fact, important to remember that sometimes it is we, who call ourselves disciples of Jesus and Mary, who provide the ingratitude and lack of love through our lives, through our moral decisions that become a betrayal of Love. This is important to recognize not only out of a necessary humility but also in order to better understand a spirituality of reparation. Reparation, in its truest sense, means making amends to the Sacred Heart and the Immaculate Heart for both our sins and those of our brothers and sisters. Because we make amends for our sins, through acts of reparation, we are saying to Jesus and Mother Mary that we are sorry for our sins and shortcomings and telling them that we love them and want to make it up to them for how we have hurt them.

When the great Capuchin saint, mystic, and stigmatic Padre

Pio heard confessions, he was often found to be in tears and explaining to the penitent how that person's sins were a betrayal of Love. This pastoral response is so important to internalize because what Padre Pio was trying to communicate is that a person's sins are not just a violation of an abstract set of moral codes or obligations but a betrayal of a relationship, the relationship with Jesus Crucified, who is Love and who suffered because of these sins. For too often a penitent can treat his or her sins with such a superficial mentality, a mentality of reading off a list of broken moral codes, not realizing how the sins, and especially the lack of effort in battling these sins, is a betrayal of a relationship; how Jesus and Mother Mary are hurt by the lack of effort and by our decisions to choose sin over them.

When a man and a woman are married, they take sacred vows to each other, promising to honor the other through a life of fidelity and love, in good times and in bad, in sickness and in health. Therefore, when moral temptations arise, the memory of the spouse, the fidelity that was promised to them, the love that one should have for the other, should be the incentive to fight and overcome those temptations. What is essentially being honored, through the interior battle and decision to overcome, is another person; it is the sacredness of the relationship with that person.

Through our baptism, we are also invested into a sacred relationship. We are made spiritual sons and daughters of God the Father. We receive adopted sonship through the sacred graces that come from the Cross, and thus from the suffering and death of Jesus Christ. Therefore, when we say No to sin, when we make the effort to fight moral temptations, when we ask for the grace to overcome, we are being true to a Person, to a living relationship. We are saying through our lives and the decisions that we make that His sacrifice meant something; it meant everything. And because He suffered for me, I am willing to fight for Him.

Co-Redemption for the Conversion of Sinners

The aspect of co-redemption is important to understand in a spirituality of reparation as well. Because we make amends for the sins of our brothers and sisters, through acts of reparation we are able to become co-redeemers with Jesus and Mary, offering our prayers and sacrifices also for the conversion of sinners. Spiritually, this sacred reality is connected to our baptism. All Christians, in virtue of their baptism, have a special participation with Christ in His identity as priest, prophet, and king. Part of the priestly identity includes offering sacrifice. For most Christians this will not come through ministerial priesthood, where the sacrifice of the Mass is offered—as only an ordained man can offer such a sacrifice—but there will still be a connection to the Mass. In a similar way that each Mass is offered by a priest for a specific intention, as a wellspring of abundant graces for someone who needs them, Christians can (through the royal priesthood of Jesus Christ living within them, as members of the mystical body), offer their prayers and sufferings for the intentions of others as an act of intercession that can provide great graces.

Theologically, this can be explained through the distinction between what is called "objective redemption" and "subjective redemption." Objective redemption pertains to the meritorious suffering and death of Jesus at Calvary, which won infinite graces for the human race. Subjective redemption, however, pertains to how those graces will be distributed throughout the world to assist souls. Our Lady, as mediatrix of graces, helps through her special mediation to distribute those graces.[25] However, out of His

---

[25] Pope St. John Paul II, as well as a number of Mariologists, makes the claim that Our Lady's special participation in the Redemption of Jesus Christ extends to Objective Redemption as well. "The collaboration of Christians in salvation takes place after the Calvary event, whose fruits they endeavor to spread by prayer and sacrifice. Mary, instead, co-operated in the event itself and in the role of mother; thus her co-operation embraces the whole of Christ's saving work. She alone was associated in this way with the redemptive sacrifice that merited the salvation of all mankind. In union with Christ and in submission

goodness and generosity, the Lord allows us, human creatures, to participate in this subjective redemption as well, to help our Mother's mission. Our Lady, as she did in Fatima, asks for our help and participation, for our prayers and sacrifices. It is through those prayers and sacrifices that graces from the Cross are accessed and distributed throughout the earth to aid poor sinners who are most in need. Hence, Jesus and Mary are allowing us an immensely important role to play in the salvation of the world.

The First Five Saturdays Devotion

Years after the Marian apparitions of 1917, the remaining Fatima visionary, now Sister Lucia living in the convent, continued to receive visionary experiences of Our Lady. One of the most important of these visionary experiences, which resulted in the spreading of a significant devotion of reparation to the Immaculate Heart of Mary, transpired on December 10, 1925.

Sister Lucia experienced a special apparition. With the Child Jesus by her side, Our Lady appeared in Sister Lucia's room. Placing one hand on Lucia's shoulder, Our Lady extended her other hand, in which she held a heart covered with sharp thorns. Then the Child Jesus spoke, saying, "Have compassion on the Heart of Your Most Holy Mother. It is covered with the thorns [with] which ungrateful men pierce it at every moment, and there is no one to remove them with an act of reparation."[26] After her Son, Our Lady spoke:

---

to him, she collaborated in obtaining the grace of salvation for all humanity." This theological position would make sense in terms of Our Lady's unique role as New Eve, being the only other person, besides Jesus, who was born without original sin and lived without actual sin, the unique purity of her soul having a unique participation in His Redemption. Pope St. John Paul II, Papal Audience, April 9, 1997, §2, https://www.vatican.va/content/john-paul-ii/en/audiences/1997/documents/hf_jp-ii_aud_09041997.html.

[26] Heimann, Fatima, 70.

My daughter, look at my Heart encircled with the thorns [with] which ungrateful men pierce it at every moment by their blasphemies and ingratitude. Do you at least try to console me and announce in my name that I promise to assist at the hour of death with great graces necessary for salvation all those who, on the first Saturday of five consecutive months, go to confession and receive Holy Communion, recite the Rosary and keep me company for a quarter of an hour while meditating on the mysteries of the Rosary with the intention of making reparation to me.[27]

With this significant apparition the First Five Saturdays devotion was born. If we delineate the devotion into four parts, they appear as follows:

1. Going to confession

2. Receiving Holy Communion

3. Praying five decades of the Rosary

4. Keeping Mother Mary company for fifteen minutes while meditating on the mysteries of the Rosary

Furthermore, these spiritual practices should be performed *with the intention* of making reparation to the Immaculate Heart of Mary.

It is a beautiful act, to wake up on a Saturday morning for five consecutive months, holding in one's heart the thought of our Mother's sorrows and knowing that today *I can make reparation*; today *I can console her suffering heart*. There is such loving intimacy in this act of devotion toward her, as the day is dedicated to loving her, especially in her pain.

Consider again the power of the words spoken by the Child

---

[27] Heimann, *Fatima*, 70.

Jesus as He pleaded with Sister Lucia to have compassion "on the Heart of Your Most Holy Mother," for it is covered with the thorns with "which ungrateful men pierce it at every moment, and there is no one to remove them with an act of reparation." These painful words reveal that, as Mother of the Mystical Body, as our Spiritual Mother, Our Lady is so intimately united to the human race that she experiences hurt, being pierced "at every moment" because of the sins and ingratitude of mankind. In a mystical way, she continues to suffer.

However, the words of the Child Jesus offer hope by allowing us to understand that we can console our Mother's sorrowful Heart. What an absolute honor this is.

While the First Five Saturdays devotion has a certain structure and timeframe, and has become a popular expression of a spirituality of reparation, it is also important to recognize that acts of reparation to both Jesus and Mary can be offered each and every day. The earlier messages of Fatima, both the angelic and the Marian, stressed the importance of making reparation through prayer and sacrifice, and of making of everything that one can a sacrifice to God as an act of reparation for the sins by which He is offended and for the conversion of sinners. That is, reparation can be a daily call, a daily expression of one's spiritual life. A person does not need to wait for the first Saturday of the month in order to interiorly offer a holocaust of love to God or to the Mother of God to console their Hearts. Let us consider a few ways in which such regular acts of reparation can be made.

Reparation through Prayer and Adoration

The Eucharist is the sacrament of Jesus's love. There is a special intimacy, therefore, that a soul receives from Eucharistic adoration, from contemplatively resting in the presence of the Eucharistic Lord and being showered by the tender graces of His sweet anointing, by the inspirations that come through that still, small voice that speaks to us in the interior silence of our hearts. Jesus waits for us in the Blessed Sacrament, desiring our affection and intimacy, desiring the gift of our time. Often, we make the excuse that we do not have time for Him, for Eucharistic adoration, because there is so much to do and take care of in the day. But the truth is, we always make time for the things that we love. It is not time that we lack. It is love.

In His sweet Eucharistic presence, our Lord encounters many souls who are closed off to Him, who do not honor the gift of His presence and even treat Him like a stranger, neglected and alone. Too often this abandonment that He experiences, which started in Gethsemane and extends to the tabernacles of the world, is perpetrated by those who have the sacred honor of being His most intimate friends, His beloved priests. The sin of the Apostles, the first priests of Christ, who abandoned Him during His Passion, when in His vulnerability and poverty He needed them most, continues to this day. It is promulgated by too many priests who, seduced by the comforts of the world, have become estranged and separated from Him, turning to false idols with their time and devotion, to the tabernacle of various screens and comforts. What we spend most of our time in front of becomes our tabernacle, what we worship.

Of course, a number of good and holy priests who honor the Eucharistic Jesus still exist; they understand well that everything that they do—providing spiritual direction, hearing confessions, preaching, making pastoral visits—receives the sweet unction of supernatural grace through the fruit of prayer. They are filled with the power and anointing of the Holy Spirit through the time that they spend with the Eucharistic Jesus in prayer and contemplative silence, allowing Him to nourish and strengthen their souls. The vitality of grace shines through a man who has a living relationship with Jesus Christ.[28] This is the kind of priest who doesn't just

---

[28] Fr. Jacques Philippe articulates: "More than intellectual reflection, or a search

know *about* Jesus through the study of theology, but who knows Jesus personally with an experiential intimacy through the school of prayer and the countless hours spent in the classroom of the spiritual life that is the Eucharistic chapel.

There is, however, great need to make reparation for the ways that Jesus has been neglected, forsaken, and abandoned by too many souls, priestly and laity, in churches and tabernacles throughout the world. There is great need to make reparation for the ways that the Eucharist has been blasphemed, for how few Catholics actually believe in the physical presence of Jesus Christ in the Holy Sacrament. There is great need to make reparation for the priests who no longer believe and no longer celebrate the sacred liturgy of the Eucharist with reverence, rushing through their sacred duties as if God Almighty were not actually present in their hands.

We make reparation to the Eucharistic Lord by coming to Him, by showing Him with our time that His presence matters; by praying before the Blessed Sacrament not only for our intentions and those of our loved ones but also with the intention of reparation, telling the humble Lord that we desire to make reparation with our presence for those who do not believe, do not adore, do not trust, and do not love the Eucharistic Jesus, echoing in our hearts the prayer of the Angel of Fatima.

Even if one's parish does not have exposition of the Blessed Sacrament available frequently—that is, scheduled times of Eucharistic adoration—if ever at all (some parishes, unfortunately, do not), then one can certainly come to church and pray before the tabernacle, as the Eucharistic Jesus is present within and the graces of His love still flow from the sacred encounter. The act of visiting Him becomes an act of love. It is saying to Jesus, despite

---

for new or original ideas, or brilliant study, prayer is the secret of preaching." *Priestly Fatherhood: Treasure in Earthen Vessels* (New York: Scepter Publishers, 2021), 152.

the ingratitude and emptiness which surrounds Him, "My soul is here to console and love You," offering Jesus the thanksgiving, praise, and adoration that He deserves from the world.

Our Lady is mystically present with us in those moments, as she is the greatest adorer of her Son. In fact, it is she who often leads us to adore Him. "The Blessed Virgin calls us to sanctuary. She invites us to follow Jesus into the lonely places of the desert, the wilderness, or the top of a mountain. There we are nurtured in the intimate love of God who knows us, loves us, and serves us. There we discern His divine will. In sanctuary, we return to Gethsemane and Golgotha to contemplate the Suffering Servant," Fr. Anthony Buś explains.[29]

Fr. Anthony's words speak deep truths, especially how when we enter sanctuary and come before the Eucharistic Lord, we are returning to Gethsemane and Golgotha. We observed, in a previous chapter, how an eminent aspect of medieval Franciscan spirituality was asking Our Lady for the grace of suffering with her at the foot of the Cross. She meets us there. At the tabernacle, Jesus is also often abandoned. But Mother Mary waits for us, as she did before the Cross. As she did with John and the Magdalen, and a small group of women, Mother Mary desires to bring more souls to Him in the midst of His loneliness, to bring the adorers that will make reparation to Jesus's Sacred Heart, in the process consoling her Immaculate Heart.

The reality is that when we come to the tabernacle, when we kneel or rest before the Blessed Sacrament, it is a relationship that is being nourished and deepened in the most intimate parts of our souls. It is not just we who are afforded the unspeakably sublime chance to offer consolation to Jesus and His Mother, but as Fr. Anthony rightly explains, we too "are consoled in our loneliness, and we find empathy when we have been abandoned,

---

[29] Anthony Buś, *A Mother's Plea: Lifting the Veil in Sanctuary* (Stockbridge, MA: Marian Press, 2008), 206.

betrayed, or rejected. We unite our sufferings to His, and rest in His compassion."[30]

Reparation through Fasting

In her apparitions and messages, Our Lady often calls us to a deeper spirituality. That includes a spirituality of fasting, so central to living out penance and offering sacrifices. There is an ancient Christian tradition of fasting. Not only is fasting pervasively present in the Bible, both Old Testament and New, seen in the lives of central figures, from the prophet Daniel to John the Baptist to Jesus Himself, but it was also a widely present practice among early and medieval Christians. The early Christian text the *Didache*, believed to be based on the teachings of the twelve Apostles and thus communicating the spiritual practices of the early Church, explains that Christians should fast on bread and water Wednesdays and Fridays. Wednesdays because that is the day that, traditionally, is acknowledged as the day when Judas betrayed Jesus, and Friday because of the Lord's Crucifixion and death on that sacred day. Many medieval Christians even extended the fasting to Saturday in honor of Our Lady, Saturdays being liturgically celebrated in her honor.

Whether one fasts on bread and water, or from meat and sweets, or from alcohol or technology, those sacrificial acts of penance can be offered up in a spirit of reparation. The spiritual power of fasting can be explained through what I like to call the three I's of fasting: Intimacy, Intercession, and Interior Freedom. Let us consider these.

First, there is an intimacy that is present both in the sacrificial suffering that fasting entails and in the offering of reparation. When one is suffering because of the fast, feeling—as one possibility—those hunger pains, then that sacrifice can be offered in

---

[30] Buś, *A Mother's Plea*, 206.

union with the Passion of Jesus Christ. There is an intimacy here with the Lord because one gets to partake, even in a small way, in the sufferings of Jesus, the interior holocaust of self-denial that the fasting provides becomes a participation in His Crucifixion, an act of crucified love. There are few things as intimate as suffering with the one that you love. There is also intimacy in the offering of reparation. Whether one is offering their fasting in reparation to the Sacred Heart or to the Immaculate Heart or to both Jesus and Mary, the devotee is essentially saying: I love you so much, beloved Jesus and Mary, that because of the offenses, ingratitude, and blasphemies that you've had to endure, I am willing to give up food today to make reparation and offer consolation to your precious Hearts. Heaven smiles down on such souls, who usually experience greater depths of mystical love in their interior lives than Christians who have chosen comfort over the crucified love that is the Cross.

Fasting, it is important to recognize as we speak about the merits of this practice on the level of intimacy, is a relational act. In other words, it is not something that one partakes in self-centeredly but in relation to another person. Francis of Assisi was a wonderful witness to this reality. Francis usually partook in a few Lents during a given year. That is to say, Francis had numerous periods throughout the year wherein he would enter solitude and fast and pray for forty days. Perhaps the most famous of such periods came in 1224 when, fasting and praying on Mount La Verna, Francis experienced a vision that resulted in him receiving the stigmata wounds on his body. But what is especially important to recognize in the example of Francis is that when he spent his forty-day periods of fasting, he usually offered his fast in honor of a sacred figure: whether it was the Blessed Virgin Mary, or St. Michael the Archangel, or St. Peter, or another. For Francis, his self-denial was connected to another person whom he was honoring through the sacrifice, the self-denial becoming a self-gift.

The power of such a spirituality is that these heavenly figures for whom Francis was offering his fast are important intercessors who can use the sacrifices and merits of a person on earth in order to mediate graces from heaven. Our Lady, as the primary example, is the mediatrix of all graces. Thus, in offering a fast to her, a person is not only partaking in an act of intimacy through this spiritual bouquet but also giving her permission to use the merits of the fast to mediate graces for those who need it most. This gets into the second I of fasting: Intercession.

In the Gospel when His Apostles were not able to exorcise a demon from a person, Jesus replied that certain demons can only be removed through prayer *and fasting*. Here what we see is the high intercessory value of fasting: it is a practice that can implore the grace to liberate another person from demonic strongholds. This reality is strongly connected to Our Lady's emphasis in Fatima that so many souls go to hell because there is no one to pray and sacrifice for them. One does not need to be "possessed" in order to live a life that is guided by demonic influences and temptations, is oriented toward mortal sin and ruin, and can lead to eternal damnation. Often, what can help such a person is having an intercessor, an individual who is willing to both pray and sacrifice for them, so that they may receive the grace of deeper freedom, wisdom, and conversion of heart. Without the St. Monicas of the world, we would not have the St. Augustines, and the world would be a lesser place for it.

Do you have someone in your life, someone close to you, who is struggling with addiction, perhaps to alcohol or drugs, or pornography or promiscuity; or who perhaps is struggling with atheism or agnosticism, or unhealthy occult or New Age practices, having fallen away from the faith with false beliefs; or perhaps is struggling with sexual confusion, or unforgiveness, or has a broken relationship with his family?

If so, don't just pray for them. Fast for them. Certain demons can only be removed through prayer and fasting.

Like her Son in the Gospel, Our Lady is calling us to a deeper, radical spirituality of Christian discipleship that can, through the embracement of the Cross, help work wonders and miracles of newfound freedom and deep interior conversion in the lives of others. Jesus gives us the ultimate example at Calvary of crucified love, and one of the things that His example shows us is that there is great power of grace that God bestows upon human lives when love is combined with sacrifice as an offering of mediation and intercession.

Sometimes the wonders and miracles that we desperately need to see pertain to our own lives. This is where the third I of fasting comes in: Interior Freedom. When we deny our physical senses through fasting and combine the practice with prayer, then our spiritual senses tend to come to life and we can cultivate a greater self-mastery. Whatever your struggle is, whether it is lust, anger, unforgiveness, fasting helps. The Church Fathers emphasized that if one is struggling with lust, then he should fast.

I have found in my own life that when I am fasting, temptations have less of an impact on me and difficult or abrasive situations, or persons, usually make me less angry, not bothering me as much, if at all. It feels as if fasting helps provide the grace of a spiritual armor around the mind and soul that normal temptations have difficulty penetrating. And remember, fasting is relational, not self-centered, meaning that even if you are fasting in order to cultivate a greater inner freedom and virtue in your own life, you still need to rely on the Other to do so, offering an act of surrender. That is, you need to offer your fast to Jesus and say, "Help me, Lord. Help me to overcome this vice. Help me to overcome these temptations. I am offering this fast to show You that I *want* to live for You, that I want to live righteously. I am offering this fast to show You that I want to be free, and that I love You, and that I no longer want to crucify You with my sins. But help me, Lord. Because without You, I can do nothing."

The Lord sees that you are doing everything that you possibly can in your willpower to overcome the vices and evils dominating your life, and the Lord sees that you recognize, through your poverty and vulnerability, that your willpower alone is not enough, but you must surrender and beg for the strength of His grace as well. Many people say that they are "struggling" with a vice like lust. But the truth is, they are not struggling; they are just giving in at the first temptation. The word "struggle" implies a real fight, a decision to do battle; a real effort made to overcome the strong allure of evil. Few are willing to struggle because it is easier to habitually frequent the confessional and then fall back into the sin, living a double life that can become a betrayal of love and an abuse of the sacrament, using the confessional as part of the addiction ritual. If the confessional is easily available, then I can say Yes to the sin because I will be forgiven. Such a mentality can lead a person to spending years of his life enslaved to the patterns of mortal sin because at the heart of it he doesn't *want* to be free. I see this pattern way too frequently as a priest hearing confessions. One shouldn't say that he is struggling and wants freedom when he isn't willing to fight for it.

It is when these two forces meet—the unconditional effort of the individual who is willing to embrace any difficulty to find freedom, including embracing the heroic sacrifice of fasting, and the self-awareness to know that the person cannot do it by himself but because of his poverty and vulnerability needs the grace and power of God to assist him—that the greatest miracles of interior freedom can transpire.

It is important to remember that Our Lady also told the children of Fatima that many people go to hell because of the sins of the flesh. That is not a message to take lightly. The eternal salvation of your soul is much more important than brief, passing moments of pleasure that leave a person feeling shame, guilt, and emptiness afterward. God is merciful. But we must cooperate with His grace and mercy and show Him that we are willing to fight for true love, having the Crucified Jesus and Mary, Mother of Sorrows, on the mind and heart. They have suffered so much for us, and there is no need to increase their sufferings with our sins when we have the choice to truly fight.

The Importance of Her Apparitions

Mother Mary's message of reparation comes through her apparitions; the request for the spiritual practice becomes a call from heaven. Let us conclude this chapter by considering why her apparitions are important.

In a series of fascinating interviews that Joseph Cardinal Ratzinger, many years before becoming pope, provided to the Italian journalist Vittorio Messori, he shared the following illuminating thoughts about Marian apparitions:

> No apparition is indispensable to the faith; Revelation terminated with Jesus Christ. He Himself is the Revelation. But we certainly cannot prevent God from speaking to our time through simple persons and also through extraordinary signs that point to the insufficiency of the cultures stamped by rationalism and positivism that dominate us. The apparitions that the Church has officially approved—especially Lourdes and Fatima—have their precise place in the development of the life of the Church in the last century. They show, among other things, that Revelation—still unique, concluded and therefore unsurpassable—is not yet a dead thing but something alive and vital.[31]

Whether it is the healing miracles associated with Lourdes, the miracle of the dancing sun in Fatima seen by tens of thousands

---

[31] Joseph Cardinal Ratzinger with Vittorio Messori, *The Ratzinger Report: An Exclusive Interview on the State of the Church*, trans. Salvator Attanasio and Graham Harrison (San Francisco, CA: Ignatius Press, 1985), 111.

of witnesses—believers and skeptics alike—or the image of a visionary in ecstasy experiencing a supernatural apparition of the Mother of Christ, the entire worldview of rationalism and positivism is challenged by the spiritual universe that Marian apparitions represent.

Our Lady's apparitions are important because they remind us, contemporary people, that the ancient truths of the Catholic faith, as found in the Bible and in Sacred Tradition—truths such as the Incarnation, the healing miracles, the Resurrection of Jesus, the supernatural validity of the sacraments—are not simply myths of human construction but authentic realities received from the Divine. Our Lady's apparitions show us that the supernatural is real, that God is, that the afterlife exists. Heaven is real. Hell is real. There are eternal consequences for our moral and spiritual decisions. Our lives, therefore, have deep and everlasting meaning.

In a modern world that has lost its sense of the supernatural, that has abandoned sacred realities, steeped as it is in the ideologies of secularism and rationalism and no longer believing in the Eucharist or the miraculous witness of the Gospel, Our Lady's apparitions make a statement, saying: My Son is real. The Eucharist is real. The Gospel is real. The God of the supernatural is real.

If the Mother of God can appear in the nineteenth and twentieth centuries and beyond, her supernatural presence leaving signs and wonders in the miracles that are worked by the grace of God at her apparition sites, then there is no reason why the miracles of her Son could not transpire in first-century Palestine. The miracles of the present support and vindicate the miracles of the past, pointing to their validity. When healings happen at apparition sites like Lourdes and Fatima, they happen through the power of Jesus Christ, showing that the ancient power which worked wonders in the Gospel continues to work wonders today. The Mother points to the Son. Her apparitions have called millions of people to deeper conversion and renewal of faith. Our Lady's apparitions do what private revelations are meant to do:

they lead souls to belief in public revelation, in the truth, goodness, and beauty of the Catholic faith and the sacraments.

In a conversation with Bishop Robert Barron about the state of the Church, Jordan Peterson spoke about the need for priests to preach about the adventure and cosmic drama that Christianity entails. "And this isn't hit home: the Church demands everything of you, absolutely everything. And the reason people are leaving is because that adventure isn't being put in front of them," he said, emphasizing how the challenging demands of Christianity, which bring meaning and adventure to life, are frequently not preached in favor of a more watered-down version of the faith. "You need to be engaged in something that's deeply meaningful enough to justify the suffering [of life]," Peterson continued. "Part of what happens in the story of Christ is that the only thing deep enough to justify that level of suffering is absolute immersion in a cosmic drama. And then you ask yourself, are we each immersed in a cosmic drama? And it's not so easy to say no to that. It's a life or death situation."[32]

Our Lady's apparitions, pointing to a grand narrative, the grand narrative of Christianity—that life is sacred, that our moral decisions and spiritual lives have meaning, that the afterlife is real, that angels and demons exist, that heaven and hell are real, that Christ is divine and is at the center of human existence—show us that we are all immersed in a much bigger story, a cosmic drama.

Let us now turn to a highly important piece of that drama, a piece which shows us an essential side of Mother Mary's identity and our own role and responsibility in helping her advance the mission of her Son: the drama of the spiritual warfare.

---

[32] Deflate, "THIS Is Why People Are Leaving the Church! (The Peterson-Barron Conversation)," YouTube video, 11:59, April 29, 2021, https://www.youtube.com/watch?v=BVrLqpt0APo.

❧ Chapter 7 ❧

Warrior Queen:

Returning to the Spiritual Battle

That's what the Bible wants us to know about the Queenship of Mary: she's all about the spiritual struggle, the spiritual warfare. [St.] Paul said we battle not against flesh and blood, but against powers and principalities.

—Bishop Robert Barron

The demon is so terrified of her that he will never pronounce her name. He'll say "that woman" or "she destroys me."

—Fr. Gabriele Amorth

We began this book with a simple question, "What's in a name?"

Like the late Fr. Gabriele Amorth, for decades the chief exorcist of Rome, Msgr. Stephen Rossetti, head exorcist of the Archdiocese of Washington, DC, explains that demons hate the Virgin Mary "so much that they will refuse to speak her name but refer to her only as 'that woman' or some abstraction. Her name, like Jesus', is considered holy and is itself odious to the demons and a grace for those who utter it with devotion."[1] Rossetti further explains that it "is expected that a Catholic exorcist would have a

---

[1]   Stephen J. Rossetti, *Diary of an American Exorcist: Demons, Possession, and the Modern-Day Battle against Ancient Evil* (Manchester, NH: Sophia Institute Press, 2021), 123.

strong devotion to the Blessed Virgin Mary, the Mother of Jesus. After Jesus Himself, she is the strongest ally of the exorcist."[2]

The ministry of exorcism is an ancient practice, a ritual that, as the *Catechism of the Catholic Church* explains, is "directed at the expulsion of demons or to the liberation from demonic possession through the spiritual authority which Jesus entrusted to his Church."[3] Exorcisms were performed by Jesus Himself, the greatest exorcist, who throughout the Gospels is overthrowing and dismantling the kingdom of darkness, delivering people from demons and their influence. The reality of this ministry speaks to a wider metaphysical worldview, a significant narrative that cannot be overlooked. Life is a battle between two kingdoms. And we have a responsibility, as St. Paul writes, to "Put on the whole armor of God, that you may be able to stand against the wiles of the devil. For we are not contending against flesh and blood, but against the principalities, against the powers, against the world rulers of this present darkness, against spiritual hosts of wickedness in the heavenly places" (Eph 6:11–12). The Council Fathers of Vatican II reaffirm this ageless truth, writing:

> For a monumental struggle against the powers of darkness pervades the whole history of man. The battle was joined from the very origins of the world and will continue until the last day, as the Lord has attested. Caught in this conflict, man is obliged to wrestle constantly if he is to cling to what is good, nor can he achieve his own integrity without great efforts and the help of God's grace.[4]

There are many Christians, including those within the Catholic Church, among them priests, who deny the existence of the devil

---

[2] Rossetti, *Diary of an American Exorcist*, 122.

[3] CCC §1673.

[4] Vatican II, Pastoral Constitution on the Church in the Modern World *Gaudium et Spes*, (1965), §37.

and demons, seeing their presence in the Bible more as a symbol. The Spanish exorcist Fr. José Antonio Fortea aptly explains, "Demons are personal spiritual beings, as is the chief demon, the devil. Those Christians who deny the existence of demons and say that they are merely symbols of evil are heretics. Against this false belief stand the teachings of Christ, the teachings of the Bible, and the teachings of the Church (see CCC 391–395)."[5]

There is an ancient battle that our ancestors have been participating in for centuries, a battle that we are all born into, whether we know it or not. Fr. Michael Scanlan, T.O.R., once wrote that life is a battle between two kingdoms, the Kingdom of Darkness and the Kingdom of Light, and in the end we will all be judged by how well we did as soldiers in the battle. "We are both the soldiers in the armies and the battleground upon which the war takes place. Our eternal destiny is what the war is all about."[6]

It is a battle between Christ and Lucifer, between angels and demons, between saints and the principalities and powers of darkness. Angels and demons and the spiritual realm exist. They are real, whether a person believes in them or not. Angelic spirits (both good and evil) surround us and try to influence us and our decisions, either toward the light or toward the darkness; toward the moral and spiritual good or toward vice and evil. Souls are on the line, the most precious commodity that the human person possesses, what both God and the devil seek—one for eternal happiness, the other for eternal damnation.

This is the meaning of life. Once we take our eyes off the spiritual struggle that surrounds us, we become like Plato's prisoners staring at shadows, our lives fixated on superficial and meaningless pursuits that keep us blinded from our spiritual destiny and

---

[5] Fr. José Antonio Fortea, *Interview with an Exorcist: An Insider's Look at the Devil, Demonic Possession, and the Path to Deliverance* (West Chester, PA: Ascension Press, 2006), 13.

[6] Fr. Michael Scanlan with Jim Manney, *Let the Fire Fall*, 3rd ed. (Steubenville, OH: Franciscan University Press, 2016), 190.

enslaved to the very idols of pleasure, pride, comfort, and materialism whose triumph over the soul, leading to spiritual death, becomes a demonic victory. Again, whether one is conscious of it or not, awake to the reality or blind to it, the battle is real and there is no way of avoiding it. To be born is to be immersed into this epic cosmic drama that has eternal consequences.

Our Lady has a significant role in this battle. An essential element to understanding her identity is that she is a spiritual warrior—in fact, as Queen Mother, thus the Warrior Queen, she is a major leader alongside her Son Christ the King and St. Michael the Archangel in the spiritual combat against the devil and his fallen angels, the demons. It is a reality that is present throughout the bookends of Scripture, from Genesis to Revelation.

In the first book of the Bible, after Adam and Eve disobey God through their sin, God tells the serpent who tempted them that there will be "enmity between you and the woman, and between your seed and her seed; he shall bruise your head, and you shall bruise his heel" (Gen 3:15). This passage is known as the *protoevangelium*, that is, the "first Gospel" or "first Good News," for it is the earliest passage in the entirety of the Bible that alludes to the coming of the Messiah. Notice that this allusion comes through the woman who will have enmity with the serpent. It is her offspring that will bring hope. The word *enmity* is important, as it implies complete and radical opposition, meaning, she who has enmity with Satan has nothing to do with him or his ways, being completely free of sin. There is an implicit support in the term for her immaculate nature, for the fact that she will be conceived and live without sin.

Chapter 12 of the Book of Revelation speaks prominently of the battle between the Woman and the dragon, again making reference to the Mother of the Messiah. "She brought forth a male child, one who is to rule all the nations with a rod of iron, but her child was caught up to God and to his throne" (Rev 12:5). Within this battle, Our Lady's spiritual maternity is acknowledged, how it is her children who are involved in the warfare. "Then the dragon was angry with the woman, and went off to make war on the rest of her offspring, on those who keep the commandments of God and bear testimony to Jesus" (Rev 12:17).

Our Lady loves us so much that she enters this battle in numerous ways in order to protect and defend her children, to fight for us. Through her ceaseless prayers, through her advocacy before the throne of God, through her apparitions where she has given so many warnings and messages to implore our conversion, through her sufferings on earth, through the exorcisms wherein she is invoked to help liberate souls from the demonic powers of darkness, she is there, fighting for us. Her love is radiantly present as a Spiritual Mother in her role as Warrior Queen.

To truly appreciate how ancient and important this spiritual war is, and to gain a richer understanding of Our Lady's role as Lucifer's archnemesis, it is essential to go back to the beginning, to how it all began. If we truly consider the origins of this spiritual struggle, it extends to time immemorial.

How the Battle Began

Chapter 12 of the Book of Revelation tells us that there is a spiritual war. It is a war that is ancient, that has been fought even before time began, originating in heaven. It is a war that has generals and soldiers, including hierarchies of ranking angels and demons. It is a war that has, at the center of the battle, the two most perfect creatures that God ever created, the Virgin Mary and Lucifer, the latter corrupted by his pride, the former elevated by her humility and perfect obedience to Christ, her *fiat*.

The battle arose in heaven between St. Michael and the holy angels against the dragon and his angels, who would become (as fallen angels) demons. The dragon is Lucifer, who was the original "light-bearer," as the etymology of his name specifies. He was created by God as a sublime and beautiful angel of light who, unfortunately, rebelled through his pride and became corrupted. The allusion to Lucifer's influence over the other angels who would follow him is represented in symbolic language, that of the dragon's tail sweeping "down a third of the stars of heaven" and hurling "them to the earth" (Rev 12:4). As fallen angels, Lucifer and his angelic followers became demons.

Thus, before the spiritual war began on earth, it was initiated as a cosmic battle in heaven. What was it, the question may be asked, that led to the fall of the angels, that led specifically the fallen angels to rebel?

Whereas angelology and demonology, the study of angels and demons, are highly speculative theological sciences, since we weren't there when the cosmic heavenly battle transpired and therefore cannot know the exact details, there are suggestions in Scripture and in the writings of the Church Fathers that point to real possibilities. The Church, technically, does not have a definitive teaching on why the angels fell. A popular explanation, however, provided by a number of Church Fathers and latter theologians as well as being implicitly present within the language of Scripture, is that the Incarnation was at the center of the controversy.

Specifically, it was the idea that the Incarnation was offensive to the pride of certain angels, Lucifer and those who chose to follow him, because as Fr. John Horgan explains, "If God revealed to the angels that His Son, the Eternal Word, would one day unite Himself in being to a human nature, a nature lower than the angels, that would mean that they would have to adore God in a form lowlier than their own."[7] This reality would have a significant impact on the relationship between angels and humans, who were yet to be created:

---

[7] Fr. John Horgan, *His Angels at Our Side: Understanding Their Power in Our Souls and the World* (Irondale, AL: EWTN Publishing, 2018), 33.

And by implication, they [the angels] would not only bend the knee (so to speak) to the Word Made Flesh but would have to assist man, the as-yet-uncreated lower creature, in taking *his special place* in God's Kingdom. Their own intelligence, strength, and power would be directed to cooperating with God in this plan in which they did not have the highest place, despite being the first created and despite many superior gifts in their angelic nature.[8]

It is in the context of the Book of Revelation that we see Scriptural support for the theory that the Incarnation was at the center of the war and the fall of the angels. Informally titled in many Bible translations as "The Woman and the Dragon," chapter 12 depicts the two events, the fall of the angels and the Incarnation, as being successively (and perhaps intrinsically) connected, explaining that the dragon's "tail swept down a third of the stars of heaven, and cast them to the earth. And the dragon stood before the woman who was about to bear a child, that he might devour her child when she brought it forth" (Rev 12:4).

Of course, we use the word "successively" here as representing a symbolic pattern—one event leading to another, having a causal relationship with the other—and not in the strict sense of the word of one event being historically preceded by another, as heaven, in its eternity, exists outside of time and not in successive correlation to historical events on the earth like the Incarnation. The angels would know of the Incarnation before the event ever happened, even before the human race was created.

Certain facts about the sin of the angels are without dispute. The sin that the angels were guilty of had to be of a spiritual nature. In other words, it could not have been a fleshly sin, such as lust or gluttony, since angels as pure spirits do not have physical bodies and, therefore, could not have committed corporal vices. Thus,

---

8 Horgan, *His Angels at Our Side*, 33–34.

the sin was either pride or envy, or very likely both—the pride being addressed toward God, whom they refused to adore and obey but wanted to resemble in power; the envy toward humans, whom they refused to serve.

In his work *Angels and Demons*, the French Dominican, Fr. Serge-Thomas Bonino, O.P., explains the core connection between the fall of the angels and the fall of the human race. "The diabolical suggestion whispered to Eve—'You will be like gods' (Gn 3:5)—is like an echo of the angel's sin of pride."[9] On the other hand, it may be argued, isn't it a good thing to want to be like God? After all, are we not called to resemble Him and be Godlike? Did not Christ become man so that we may be divinized?

Fr. Bonino clarifies, "In fact there are certain aspects of the divine perfection that are communicable and that a spiritual creature can legitimately aim to attain (to be wise and good), but there are others that are proper to God and incommunicable (such as being the Creator of heaven and earth) and that it would be sinful to desire. Now the angel wanted something of this second type."[10]

Sometimes the drama of this reality is most tragically represented by our great poets. John Milton in *Paradise Lost* famously depicted Lucifer as a proud angel of light who told God that it is better to reign in hell than to serve in heaven. As Fr. Bonino points out about Lucifer, "He preferred to remain first in an inferior order than to become one among others in a superior order."[11] The gravity of his pride, unwilling to serve God and His plans in humility, is personified in this decision, a decision that was free yet corrupted his nature, a resemblance of how sin corrupts and deforms our spiritual nature by distancing us from God.

Notice here the great contrast to Our Lady. Lucifer represents

---

9   Serge-Thomas Bonino, O.P., *Angels and Demons: A Catholic Introduction*, trans. Michael J. Miller (Washington, DC: The Catholic University of America Press, 2016), 205.

10   Bonino, *Angels and Demons*, 205.

11   Bonino, *Angels and Demons*, 206.

the axiom of *non serviam*. "I will not serve." Our Lady's very identity represents the opposite, her being is her *fiat*, her life is her
mission to serve and honor God. "Behold, I am the handmaid of
the Lord." Whereas Eve accepted the serpent's temptation to "be
like gods," Mary accepted the angel's invitation to be the handmaid of the Lord. In the Latin, the very proclamation of the angel
Gabriel, *Ave Maria*, constitutes the metaphysical inversion of Eve,
as "Ave" spelled backwards is "Eva." And Mary is the beginning
in God's salvific process of undoing the sin that began with Eve
and her tempter, the serpent, who is the devil. She is the archnemesis of the devil. They are polar opposites who, interestingly,
share certain fundamental commonalities, at least in terms of who
Lucifer was created to be. Fr. Fortea explains:

- Lucifer is the most perfect creature by *nature*;
  Mary, the most perfect creature by *grace*.

- Lucifer corrupted himself by *disobedience*;
  Mary sanctified herself by *obedience*.

- Lucifer wanted to be king, refusing to serve,
  and in the end became nothing; Mary wanted
  to be nothing, desiring to serve, and in the
  end was crowned Queen of heaven.[12]

Fr. Fortea continues by explaining that there is even a parallel-
ism in their titles, the "Angelic Star of the Morning" (Lucifer) and
the "Star of the Morning of the Redemption" (Mary). The reference to Lucifer, whose name means "light-bearer," as being called
Morning Star is scripturally founded in an allusion in the Book
of the Prophet Isaiah: "How you are fallen from heaven, O Day
Star, son of Dawn! How you are cut down to the ground, you
who laid the nations low! You said in your heart, 'I will ascend
to heaven; above the stars of God I will set my throne on high'"

---

[12] Fortea, *Interview with an Exorcist*, 43.

(Isa 14:12–13). Msgr. Rossetti explains that in the context of this passage, St. Jerome's Vulgate Bible translates "Morning Star" as "Lucifer," which "a number of Church Fathers identified as Satan."[13]

There is some debate among exorcists as to whether Satan and Lucifer are the same demon. Fr. Gabriele Amorth, for example, argued that they are two distinct demons.[14] Another way of understanding the two names, however, is in reference to the same demon but within different states of his existence. Therefore, "Lucifer," that is, "light-bearer," would signify not a proper name but the state from which the devil fell, as God's brightest and most perfect angel, whereas "Satan," a word that etymologically signifies "adversary" or one who obstructs or plots against another, would signify his current state.

Fr. Fortea continues to articulate the differences between Lucifer and the Blessed Virgin Mary; in the process we see two destinies that are eternally intertwined, particularly by the radically different paths that each took in the great battle of good versus evil, in the spiritual and cosmic war that surrounds the human race and the heavenly and demonic powers:

- The first star, Lucifer, fell from the angelic firmament; the second star, Mary, was elevated.

- The first star, which was spirit, fell to the earth; the second star, which was human, ascended to heaven.

- Lucifer did not want to accept the Son of God made man; the Blessed Virgin Mary welcomed Him in her womb.

- Lucifer is a spiritual being who ended up making himself worse than a beast (without ever ceasing to be spiritual); Mary is a human

---

[13] Rossetti, *Diary of an American Exorcist*, 21.

[14] Matt Baglio, *The Rite: The Making of a Modern Exorcist* (New York: Doubleday, 2009), 43.

being that ended up becoming better than an angel (without ceasing to be human).[15]

Fr. Fortea concludes, "Now there is only one 'morning star'—Mary. Not only did the first morning star fall; the second morning star shines even brighter."[16]

In fact, even during those rare exorcisms wherein the strongest of all demons, Lucifer, is present, possessing a person, the sacred presence of Mary overpowers him. Let us turn to this reality by considering the testimony of exorcists who have constantly been witness to the power of her presence against the evil one.

Our Lady in the Ministry of Exorcism

Msgr. Rossetti shares of the experience of encountering Lucifer during the ministry of exorcism, explaining that "when Lucifer shows up, he is typically surrounded by Hell's princes and many, many others. This is ugly."[17] In one exorcism session, after exorcising a person for a year and a half, and after all the lower demons, including high-ranking ones of hell, had been cast out, "Lucifer himself finally came to the fore. His personality was unique and unmistakable. He came forward with a hiss that sounded like a snake. He was not like the lower demons, who were often superficially boastful, adolescent and shallow" but was "brilliant, cunning, measured, and deadly. Lower demons cower in the presence of a priest, but Lucifer did not."[18] This was a scare tactic, a senior exorcist explained, meant to intimidate and to discern whether there is any lack of confidence in the exorcist, which the demons would exploit and pursue.

It was a difficult spiritual battle, but as Msgr. Rossetti makes clear, "we had the power of Heaven: the Blessed Virgin Mary, the

---

[15] Fortea, *Interview with an Exorcist*, 44.

[16] Fortea, *Interview with an Exorcist*, 44.

[17] Rossetti, *Diary of an American Exorcist*, 19.

[18] Rossetti, *Diary of an American Exorcist*, 20.

saints and angels, and, of course, Jesus Himself. We couldn't lose."[19] Although Lucifer had a strong army, which included high-ranking demons whose names and personalities are recognized by exorcists as princes of hell, as well as hundreds of other demons, "I invoked the Blessed Virgin Mary and prayed the Church's official Rite of Exorcism, with our lay team praying litanies. The 'King of Hell' screamed and writhed like all the rest" and, eventually, "as with all the others, the power of Christ cast him out."[20]

During another case of possession, also a rare one wherein Lucifer was present, Msgr. Rosetti shares that Our Lady appeared toward the end of the exorcism and cast out the evil one. "Whenever she appears, bearing the light of Christ, demons flee. There is no true exorcist or exorcism team that does not rely heavily on Mary. In both the old and new Rite of Exorcism, the invocation of Mary is significant. She is our Light Bearer; she is our Morning Star."[21]

It is moving, at times, to consider accounts of how Our Lady's light, reflecting the splendor of Christ's light like no one else, has been able to help liberate suffering souls from demonic torment. The Italian exorcist Fr. Francesco Bamonte dealt with a difficult case of demonic possession wherein a woman named Beatrice had to undergo weekly exorcisms for a two-year period before she was finally liberated from the possession. When the deliverance came after the final exorcism session, Beatrice testified to how instrumental Our Lady's role was in her liberation. There was a significant moment during one of the last exorcisms, she shares:

> All of a sudden (I don't remember the sequence of the events; maybe it was when the exorcist invoked Mary), I felt hit by a huge wave of a very bright white light—it

[19] Rossetti, *Diary of an American Exorcist*, 20.
[20] Rossetti, *Diary of an American Exorcist*, 20.
[21] Rossetti, *Diary of an American Exorcist*, 121.

was all encompassing, a light that I could perceive and feel as well, and it gave me a sensation of very sweet peace while for the demon it provoked atrocious pain.

Once again I felt like I was splitting, dividing between my own sensations and "his." If I closed my eyes I could see in my mind's eye that we were in a deep shadow and so I knew that the light that was embracing me was a spiritual one. Closing my eyes again, I could also perceive that this same light was stabbing the eyes of the monster like a thousand swords. Meanwhile the monster was screaming, moving like crazy, saying that the veil of Mary (whom he referred to as "that one") was suffocating him and causing him a huge amount of pain, to the point of causing him to go into terrible, indescribable spasms.[22]

When her spiritual liberation was complete and the suffering finally ended, the formerly possessed woman shared that while "I was crying tears of joy, I started to thank the Lord and the Immaculate Virgin, which I will continue to do for as long as I live."[23]

An additionally interesting element about the ministry of exorcism and the presence of the Virgin Mary is that, at times, there are moments within an exorcism when even demons can reveal sacred truths about Mary, including deeply edifying truths. A person, of course, needs to be careful as to how much can be trusted when considering the testimony of demons! Fr. Michael Baker explains the matter well, articulating, "We find that the demons themselves, whether they are forced to speak by the command of the exorcist, or are compelled by the very presence of the Blessed Virgin Mary herself, confirm core truths that the Church believes and exorcistic tradition holds in regards to

---

[22] As quoted in Baglio, *The Rite*, 199–200.

[23] Baglio, *The Rite*, 200.

the person of Mary and the role she plays in this particular ministry."[24] At the same time, caution must be used and a spiritual litmus test of discernment considered of whether or not what the demons express, in their utterances, does not contradict the truths of the Catholic faith, as revealed through the deposit of faith. Fr. Baker clarifies: "And while we can't ascertain truth or establish and develop doctrine based off of the testimony of demons, who as followers of the father of lies, who 'was a murderer from the beginning, and had nothing to do with truth, because there is no truth in him' [Jn 8:44]; to the degree that their words correspond with already established truths held by the Church, they can serve as further confirmation of those truths."[25]

Fr. Bamonte explains how special such moments can be during an exorcism, particularly when the Mother of God is present in the midst of the demons and they are forced, under divine command, to testify to the truth of her sublime and holy dignity:

> These moments are extraordinarily touching, because the demons (finding themselves blinded by so much splendor that for them is very painful) are obliged to witness to the extraordinary dignity of the Mother of God amongst all creatures, human and angelic. The demons must affirm the whole truth concerning Mary and admit their complete impotence before the desires of her who God, omnipotent by nature, having proclaimed her the Queen of the Universe, has rendered "omnipotent by grace." There is, then, a curious alternating between demons using highly vulgar and violently scornful language, followed by great expressions of catechesis together with the sweetest praises of the Virgin Mary, that the demons

---

[24] Michael A. Baker, "Maternal Mediation: The Role of the Blessed Virgin Mary in the Ministry of Exorcism" (unpublished paper, Franciscan University of Steubenville, November 21, 2017), 11.

[25] Baker, "Maternal Mediation," 11–12.

(to their chagrin and with great personal disgust) are forced to pronounce.[26]

Such "great expressions of catechesis," as Fr. Bamonte puts it, can be immensely insightful about realities pertaining to the spiritual life and the life of the Church.

Consider, for example, the famous case of Anneliese Michel, a German girl who underwent a series of exorcisms in 1976. Fr. Fortea co-authored a book with Lawrence LeBlanc on the possession of Anneliese Michel.[27] Within the book, the authors include a transcript of the audio tapes which recorded exorcism sessions, including the manifestations and words of the demons. At times, these transcripts are deeply insightful.

At one point, one of the demonic voices is complaining about Anneliese's sister and her devotion to Our Lady of Fatima. "That other one (Gertraud, Anneliese's sister) goes down there to Portugal and preaches of that one (Virgin Mary) and speaks of the apparitions in 1917. No one believes in them today. That one is taking too many from me."[28] Notice here not only the demon's reluctance toward the Virgin Mary ("that one"), refusing to speak her name, but also the power of a Catholic speaking about and promoting Our Lady's apparitions as a means of reaching souls, to the point that the demon can say that too many are being taken from his grasp. Let us learn from this when opportunities in our lives come up to promote her apparitions.

There are significant shortcomings that the demons claim about many priests and religious, particularly a noticeable worldliness, emphasizing that the "religious in the monasteries watch

---

[26] As quoted in Baker, "Maternal Mediation," 12. For original source, see Francesco Bamonte, *The Virgin Mary and the Devil in Exorcisms* (Milan: Paoline Editorale Libri, 2014), 37.

[27] Fr. Jose Antonio Fortea and Lawrence E. U. LeBlanc, *Anneliese Michel: A True Story of a Case of Demonic Possession—Germany 1976* (self-pub, 2019).

[28] Fortea and LeBlanc, *Anneliese Michel*, 115.

television and do not pray enough" and, in connection to the importance of devotion to the Rosary: "The Rosary, they do not think it is modern. Even the parish priest does not recite it. He recites the Rosary once a week, and believes to have worked a miracle having done so. Every day! No! I say nothing! How I wish the One up there did not exist! [(Mother of God)]."[29] We who are priests and religious should especially take such messages with a cue of self-examination, and not ignore the gravity of the matter, particularly the responsibility that we have before God and the Mother of God, and the lives that we are being called to serve.

Of course, what is happening in such cases—demonic manifestations that are able to utter truths—is as ancient as the Scriptures themselves. After all, it is perhaps a holy irony that in the Gospels it is, quite often, the demons who publicly proclaim the most important sacred truths, especially those pertaining to the identity of Christ. "In the synagogue there was a man who had the spirit of an unclean demon; and he cried out with a loud voice, 'Ah! What have you to do with us, Jesus of Nazareth? Have you come to destroy us? I know who you are, the Holy One of God'" (Luke 4:33–34).

Sometimes, God uses the manifestation of the devil and his demons by using the enemy as an unwitting ally to aid the Lord in His sacred work. Consider the story of one priest.

In his important book *The Priests We Need to Save the Church*, Kevin Wells shares the story of a priest who lived a very lukewarm, worldly, and prideful life, not having a serious spiritual life and no real devotion to the Blessed Virgin Mary, not even knowing how to pray the Rosary. He was a man who ministered at a trendy parish in Washington, DC, wherein some of the most famous, pro-choice Catholic politicians were his admirers. They admired him for his oratorical skills, his mannerisms, his wit and intelligence, and the fact that this priest would never speak to them—or,

---

[29] Fortea and LeBlanc, *Anneliese Michel*, 116.

at best, remain ambiguous—about sensitive moral topics, such as abortion, gay marriage, and matters of sexual morality.

The attention that he was getting, and the pride that it brought him, was more important to this priest than the at times unpopular demands of speaking moral truths, whether they were in season or out of season, for the betterment of his flock and the salvation of souls.

There were numerous experiences that the Lord used to speak to the conscience of this priest, allowing him moments of self-examination and honest reflection in considering whether he was living as he should be. When he was invited to the home of an old friend from his seminary days, a woman who was now married, had kids, and was raising her family in a small farming community, he felt "an unusual depth of warmth. . . . This feeling struck his core."[30] The family was living a lifestyle that this priest thought reflected "the old way of Catholicism."[31] They prayed the Rosary together as a family, they attended holy Mass each day, the children were obedient and happy, his friend's husband was humble and hardworking, and his friend "seemed bathed in a peace that flowed into every room she entered."[32] It was a radiant witness of a family that authentically lived out their Catholic faith. When they dropped to their knees to pray the Rosary together, it was then, Wells explains, "that a foreign voice seemed to awaken within him, one that began calling him home to a purity and life of grace he did not know."[33]

Another significant moment of grace came when this priest was transferred to a small country parish in a remote area of the state. He was introduced to the priest he would be replacing and had the chance to live alongside the man before he was officially

[30] Kevin Wells, *The Priests We Need to Save the Church* (Manchester, NH: Sophia Institute Press, 2019), 80.
[31] Wells, *The Priests We Need*, 81.
[32] Wells, *The Priests We Need*, 80.
[33] Wells, *The Priests We Need*, 81.

relocated. In this priest and in his parish, he experienced "a different spiritual universe." Wells tells the story:

> He repeatedly saw the priest rise before dawn to make a daily Holy Hour. The priest wore an easy smile, had a bushy beard, and dressed in a long cassock that whipped when he played soccer and baseball with kids in the schoolyard. He seemed to always be in the chapel, praying the Rosary, poring over Scripture, or busy with a work of charity. He watched the priest celebrate Mass with a mystic's reverence. He saw a man who resembled Jesus. . . . "I saw that what he had drew me. He had a stability to him. His prayer life consistently came first in his life. Here was a priest who prepared his own soul before he tried to present the Faith to others. Prayer and devotion were always first for him."[34]

While these were all important experiences that God was using to help this priest change his life and reform the way that he was living out his priesthood, there was still something missing. He started celebrating the Mass with greater reverence, praying the Rosary, became a spiritual director to high school kids, and increased his prayer life substantially. Yet "he still felt himself adrift. The Catholic devotions didn't feel connected to his soul."[35] It wasn't until the demonic entered the picture that God truly awoke in this priest's soul a sacred and horrifying awareness to the reality of his situation and the reality that surrounds human existence:

> One evening, a devout teenage girl who was considering religious life told him she was seeing monsters. Within

---

[34] Wells, *The Priests We Need*, 82.
[35] Wells, *The Priests We Need*, 82.

a few days, it was determined by the large city's chief exorcist that a wild chorus of demons had taken possession of her soul. Satan didn't want to let this girl go; he wasn't budging. So, over the course of the next year and a half, this priest assisted the exorcist to help drive out the demons that had infested and seized control over this worn-out young woman. Throughout this time, Satan occasionally unmasked the priest's shortcomings and mocked him. It was humiliating; he had nowhere to run or hide.[36]

The priest would later testify: "There is an intensity of impact on the human soul when it is confronted by demons, when Satan stares you down. When you see demons and what they're capable of, there comes the reality that there is most certainly a hell. Becoming aware of this dimension changed everything in my priesthood. I'll never go back to where I was. I'm just going to be a priest from now on—a real priest."[37]

"Today, all that perverted his priesthood is gone," Wells writes. "He's no longer the same man or the same priest. Nothing is the same now or will be again—the long thorns of pride and distortion have been pulled out. When more than nine hundred demons took possession of a pure soul he had been spiritually directing—some of whom called out his hidden sins, habits, and secrets in the voice of a leviathan—he came to see that hell was real and that he might one day reside there."[38]

---

[36] Wells, *The Priests We Need*, 83.

[37] Wells, *The Priests We Need*, 83. Similarly, Fr. Giancarlo Gramolazzo, an Italian exorcist who was the former president of the International Association of Exorcists, has said, "I learned more in performing exorcisms through prayer and faith than from my studies. The books that you read and study become something more theoretical; you don't get inside the world of faith. When you perform an exorcism, however, you have to enter into this world; you get in touch with the supernatural." As quoted in Baglio, *The Rite*, 80.

[38] Wells, *The Priests We Need*, 77.

"I knew I needed to change radically," the priest said. "There's no going back to the old, happy, simpleminded priestly way. Today, I am a priest who strives for holiness and wants to save souls. I've glimpsed the supernatural world. In that world, there are hideous creatures."[39]

The Ark of the Covenant and the Spiritual Battle

To have a better understanding of Our Lady's role in battling the demonic, it is important to uncover the depths of this identity in Scripture. Again, the Book of Revelation is paramount here. Whereas the most famous line of chapter 12 of Revelation is the first verse—"A great sign appeared in heaven, a woman clothed with the sun, with the moon under her feet, and on her head a crown of twelve stars"—a verse that is rich with robust and multi-layered symbolism, it cannot be fully appreciated or understood if one does not connect it to the verse that preceded the chapter, that of Revelation 11:19. Remember, the Scriptures were not originally written with chapters and verses; these division markers came much later, in the sixteenth century. Thus, it is likely that certain sections of the Bible were not meant to be divided but can be better understood, in their theological continuity, when read together. Consider, therefore, what theological depths we can see when Revelation 11:19 and 12:1 are read as parts of a whole picture (instead of separate chapters):

> Then God's temple in heaven was opened, and the ark of his covenant was seen within his temple; and there were flashes of lightning, loud noises, peals of thunder, an earthquake, and heavy hail. And a great sign appeared in heaven, a woman clothed with the sun, with the moon under her feet, and on her head a crown of twelve stars. (Rev 11:19–12:1)

---

[39] Wells, *The Priests We Need*, 77.

Notice the most important connection here, the Ark of the Covenant is seen, and that Ark is present in the form of a woman: it is the Mother of the Messiah. Therefore, as Scott Hahn explains, the "woman of the Apocalypse is the ark of the covenant in the heavenly temple: and that woman is the Virgin Mary."[40]

What is also noteworthy is that the Book of Revelation is written by St. John the Beloved, who took Our Lady into his home after the Crucifixion. He may have been, in other words—and certain Catholic mystics make this claim in their revelations—a witness to her assumption into heaven, actually seeing the woman in the sky, perhaps an experience that included a visionary component of the image of the Ark. The early Church Fathers especially depicted the image of Mary as the New Ark of the Covenant in their writings.[41]

How do we understand this type of interpretation?

It pertains to Old Testament typology: how certain images, symbols, or figures in the Old Testament typify, prophesy, foreshadow, and point to a greater figure in the New Testament who personifies the fulfillment of the Old Testament image. The Ark of the Covenant in the Hebrew Scriptures becomes a Marian symbol that points to Our Lady as the Ark of the New Covenant.

Consider the following facts.

In the Old Testament, the Ark of the Covenant, which is known as the sacred vessel carrying the presence of God, contains within itself the staff of Aaron, the tablets of the Ten

---

[40] Scott Hahn, *Hail, Holy Queen: The Mother of God in the Word of God* (New York: Image Books, 2001), 65.

[41] See Hahn, *Hail, Holy Queen*, 65–67. Hahn explains that early Church Fathers such as St. Ambrose, St. Ephrem of Syria, and St. Augustine saw the Woman of the Apocalypse—she who is identified as the Ark—as Mary while also not excluding other readings of Revelation 12, such as seeing the Woman as an allegory for the Church (in addition to identifying her as Mary). Here, what is present is a multifarious understanding of the depths of Scripture, the Fathers realizing that works as rich as Revelation have, in their penetrating gravity and symbolism, multilayered meaning.

Commandments, and the manna from heaven that God provided to feed the Israelites. The staff of Aaron represents the Levitical priesthood and foreshadows the eternal high priesthood of Jesus Christ. The tablets of the Ten Commandments represent the Word of God and foreshadow the coming of the preexistent Word who is Jesus Christ, the true Word of God, who will become man. The manna, representing bread from heaven, foreshadows the Eucharist.

Our Lady, of course, is the one who carried in her womb the eternal high priest, the living Word of God, and the Eucharistic Lord, His body that would be offered up for us on the Cross; she gave Him her own body, flesh of her flesh, and is therefore Mother of the Eucharist, the living tabernacle. As Fr. Anthony Buś poetically articulates it: "She is the *altar* that bore the sacrifice of him in whose blood we are redeemed. She is the *ark* of the New Covenant, holding within herself the *Holy of Holies*. Her Son is the jewel of the Church and is perfectly and most mysteriously perceived in the sacrifice of the Mass."[42] Even St. Francis of Assisi, in his Marian writing titled "Salutation of the Blessed

---

[42] Buś, *A Mother's Plea*, 220. Fr. Buś is the pastor of St. Stanislaus Kostka parish in Chicago, which was designated as the Sanctuary of Divine Mercy in the city in 2007 by Francis Cardinal George. The church is famous for containing one of the biggest and most beautiful Eucharistic monstrances ever created, a nine-foot-tall monstrance that is an iconic image of the Blessed Virgin Mary as the new Ark of the Covenant, holding within herself the Eucharist, which is available for adoration twenty-four hours a day in the parish. Through the exquisite work of artists Stefan Niedorezo, who did the wood carving, and Malgorzata Sawczuk, who did the gilding and served as conservator, the structural design of the iconic monstrance constitutes a bust of Our Lady that is placed upon the Ark of the Covenant, which is being adorned by angels. The church has become for many a sanctuary of solitude and contemplative silence in the midst of the busy urban city. The iconic monstrance is called "Our Lady of the Sign—Ark of Mercy." For more information and to witness the artistic beauty of the monstrance, see https://ststanschurch.org/iconic-monstrance.

Virgin Mary," offers up praise of the Madonna in the language of "Hail His Tabernacle!"[43]

It is also noteworthy that the Ark of the Covenant is associated with what, in Jewish rabbinic literature, is known as the *shekhinah*, a word referring to the dwelling of the divine presence of God. The *shekhinah* was associated with the Ark of the Covenant in the sense that the Spirit of God moved with the Ark. The connection to Our Lady is especially evident in her visitation with Elizabeth. When Mary's greeting reached Elizabeth, the Spirit of God fell upon Elizabeth and the child in her womb leaped for joy. In other words, wherever Our Lady is and wherever she goes, the Spirit of God is with her and travels with her. She is the living tabernacle. Pope St. John Paul II, in his apostolic letter *Ecclesia de Eucharistia*, puts it beautifully:

> When, at the Visitation, she bore in her womb the Word made flesh, she became in some way a "tabernacle"—the first "tabernacle" in history—in which the Son of God, still invisible to our human gaze, allowed himself to be adored by Elizabeth, radiating his light as it were through the eyes and the voice of Mary. And is not the enraptured gaze of Mary as she contemplated the face of the newborn Christ and cradled him in her arms that unparalleled model of love which should inspire us every time we receive Eucharistic communion?[44]

A very insightful connection between Our Lady's identity as the Ark of the New Covenant is established by Luke in his Gospel by making deliberate parallels to the story of David, who finds the

---

[43] Francis of Assisi, "A Salutation of the Blessed Virgin Mary," in *Francis of Assisi: Early Documents*, vol. I, *The Saint*, ed. Regis J. Armstrong, J. A. Wayne Hellmann, and William J. Short (Hyde Park, NY: New City Press, 1999), 163.

[44] John Paul II, Apostolic Letter *Ecclesia de Eucharistia* (2003), §55.

Ark in the hill country of Judah and brings it back into the holy city of Jerusalem. Scott Hahn explains, commenting on Luke's depiction in this context of Mary's visitation with Elizabeth:

> Luke's language seems to echo the account, in the second book of Samuel, of David's travels as he brought the ark of the covenant to Jerusalem. The story begins as David "arose and went" (2 Sam 6:2). Luke's account of the visitation begins with the same words: Mary "arose and went" (1:39). In their journeys, then, both Mary and David proceeded to the hill country of Judah. David acknowledges his unworthiness with the words "How can the ark of the Lord come to me?" (2 Sam 6:9)—words we find echoed as Mary approaches her kinswoman Elizabeth: "Why is this granted me, that the mother of my Lord should come to me?" (Lk 1:43). Note here the sentence is almost verbatim, except that "ark" is replaced by "mother." We read further that David "danced" for joy in the presence of the ark (2 Sam 6:14, 16), and we find a similar expression used to describe the leaping of the child within Elizabeth's womb as Mary approached (Lk 1:44). Finally, the ark remained in the hill country for three months (2 Sam 6:11), the same amount of time Mary spent with Elizabeth (Lk 1:56).[45]

What is very important to recognize in this rich biblical symbolism is that the Ark of the Covenant was often carried by the Israelites into battle. The Israelites relied on the divine presence and power that came with the Ark to help them win their battles. Here we have a foreshadowing of how important it is to take the Ark of the New Covenant into spiritual battle, to go with her, the

---

[45] Hahn, *Hail, Holy Queen*, 64.

Warrior Queen, who constitutes one of God's greatest leaders in spiritual warfare.

A majority of Marian statues depict Mary with the serpent under her foot. That depiction constitutes an essential part of her identity and cannot be ignored if one truly desires to understand her. She is the one who stomps on the serpent (Gen 3:15) and the one who does battle with the dragon (Rev 12). She is the woman who is clothed with the Sun (Rev 12:1), meaning she is clothed with immense power, the power of Christ, as it is He whom the Sun symbolizes.

Our Lady and the Priesthood: The Battle within the Church

Giving a homily to his brother priests on August 22, 2018, in the midst of the "summer of shame" that saw the release of the infamous Pennsylvania Grandy Jury Report documenting decades of clergy sexual abuse, Bishop Robert Barron emphasized that priests need to return to the spiritual battle and they need to come to an understanding of the Queenship of Mary as representing her role as a Warrior Queen, under whose command and protection they need to fight. Bishop Barron explained that, keeping true to the tradition of ancient Israel, it was the mother of the king, and not the wife, who was considered the queen, the queen mother—and both the king and the queen mother in the ancient Israelite tradition were considered warrior figures.

Bishop Barron explained that during his years as a student there was a tendency to interpret the devil as a literary figure or a symbol instead of a real spiritual force of evil. But the abuse scandals of recent decades have reconfirmed his conviction that the devil is real, for the scandals are a diabolical masterpiece; there has been no better way to undermine the work of the Church. Citing St. Paul, Bishop Barron stressed that we battle against spiritual forces, the principalities and powers of darkness, and that Our

Lady is calling us to come under the command of Christ the King and her guidance as Queen. She wants us in the spiritual battle.[46]

In his exegesis during the homily, Bishop Barron looked at the example of David as a witness to what can happen when a man loses sight of the battle in front of him. The Scriptures referenced David sinning by waking from sleep and seeing from his roof Bathsheba, who was bathing and who "was very beautiful" (2 Sam 11:2). David decided to call on her in order to have relations with her, despite the fact that she was the wife of one of his soldiers, Uriah the Hittite. This mortal sin, David's fall, happened "in the spring . . . when kings go forth to battle," but "David remained at Jerusalem" (2 Sam 11:1). And this final point, Bishop Barron articulates, is key. David was napping during a time of battle. The minute that his mind was off the fight, pleasure and power took over and led to adultery and murder, as David had Uriah killed after David impregnated Bathsheba.[47]

What the Pennsylvania Grand Jury Report represented, in the sexual sins and scandals of the past decades, was "a whole lot of Davids" who, instead of fighting in the spiritual battle and caring for their flocks, succumbed to the comforts of pleasure and power, leading to the abuse of their flocks. "When our minds are fixed on the struggle, they're fixed on what matters. We don't worry about wealth, pleasure, or power and honor."[48]

Bishop Barron concluded that in this struggle, priests need to return to the spiritual battle, realize that the devil is real, and come under the protection of Christ the King and Mary the Queen as warrior figures in the spiritual combat. "That's what the Bible wants us to know about the Queenship of Mary: she's all about

---

[46] Bishop Robert Barron, "Bishop Barron's Advice to Priests in an Age of Scandal," YouTube video, 10:13, August 22, 2018, https://www.youtube.com/watch?v=jfLrfFKT5LU.

[47] "Bishop Barron's Advice to Priests."

[48] "Bishop Barron's Advice to Priests."

the spiritual struggle, the spiritual warfare. Paul said we battle not against flesh and blood, but against powers and principalities."[49]

Because we battle against powers and principalities, the weapons of this struggle are going to be spiritual. This especially is an area where many priests have fallen short and have, therefore, gotten into trouble: the area of one's spiritual life; the area of prayer, mortification, fasting, a cultivation of interior holiness. When a priest lacks intimacy with Jesus and Mary, he will look for intimacy in the wrong places, and scandal will follow.

Monsignor John Esseff, an American priest who has been an exorcist and is considered by many a mystic, reflected how today's problem in the priesthood is rooted in the spiritual tragedy that many priests lack a serious life of prayer:

> I'm a priest sixty-five years—and I'm very strong about this. We don't have a priest shortage right now, nor do we have a shortage of vocations. What we have is a shortage of priests who pray. We have a severe crisis in our priesthood because priests are not praying. They are not fathers. If we are to do anything well as priests, it must come from prayer, but we've stopped praying.[50]

Msgr. Esseff has seen this disturbing trend of impoverished spirituality in the priesthood extend to a lack of love and reverence for the Eucharist and the Blessed Virgin Mary. "If a priest doesn't truly love the Eucharist, there's no chance for holiness. If he doesn't love Mary, there's no chance for holiness. If he doesn't love prayer, there's no chance for holiness."[51]

A major component behind the present crisis in the priesthood, connected to the spiritual poverty, is a tendency of many

---

[49] "Bishop Barron's Advice to Priests."
[50] Quoted in Wells, *The Priests We Need*, 33.
[51] Wells, *The Priests We Need*, 33.

priests to concentrate on a less important aspect of the priestly role. Instead of focusing on deepening their spiritual lives to cultivate personal holiness and authentic spiritual fatherhood for their flocks, many priests have made the administrative role of being a CEO of the parish their primary responsibility, even their idol. The writer and theologian Candace Hull explains the problem well:

> The issue for many spiritual fathers today is not that they don't work hard. Our priests work very hard, but as a priest friend recently said to me: "Too many of my brother priests are on the wrong cross. They are seeking crucifixion on the cross of administrative tasks, not prayer, Adoration, the Sacraments, ministry, and the authentic love of a spiritual father who is laying down his life as a Good Shepherd. That's why they are burned out and overwhelmed. They aren't praying enough. The Blessed Sacrament isn't central." To be crucified on the wrong cross makes it impossible to produce life-giving fruits and the salvation of souls. Parishes led by priests on the wrong cross will remain mediocre at best and spiritually oppressed at worst.[52]

It is not enough for a priest to pray the canonically required hours of his breviary and be a good administrator. In order to develop deep intimacy with Jesus and Mary, and to be a wellspring of grace who can touch people's lives with Spirit-filled preaching, teaching, words of light and supernatural meaning, he needs to spend at least an hour each day before the Blessed Sacrament in

---

[52] Constance T. Hull, "The Incredibly Fruitful Spiritual Fatherhood of Ven. Al Schwartz," Catholic Exchange, May 20, 2021, https://catholicexchange.com/the-incredibly-fruitful-spiritual-fatherhood-of-ven-al-schwartz?fbclid=IwAR0hQjGvRoLCBWo6WdsOMyP2QQSn7fmPj5dNj_dvtQ0pUvGCPbdMLiquoIw.

personal prayer. This is a prayer that is personal, more vulnerable and intimate, as heart speaks to heart, a priest giving his very self to Christ; often the intimacy is present in the silence as one simply looks at the Other in a loving, interior gaze.

It is well known that Bishop Fulton Sheen, throughout his priestly life, tried to honor the practice of making a Holy Hour every day. He made a promise on his ordination day, and he came to know the intimacy and spiritual efficacy that a daily Holy Hour had for him as a priest. Because of that Holy Hour, he wrote, "A new spirit begins to pervade our sick calls, our sermons, our confessions. The change is effected by Our Lord, Who fills our hearts and works through our hands. A priest can give only what he possesses. To give Christ to others, one must possess Him."[53]

In addition to the Eucharist, every man needs a woman in his life, and for the priest that beautiful woman is Mary, whom he needs to fight for, love, and be faithful to. In *The Priests We Need to Save the Church*, Kevin Wells rightly explains that the "priest who discards Mary permits a gulf to grow between the priest he is and the priest God wants him to become; his dismissal of Christ's Mother is an iconoclastic avoidance of his *own* possibility. Rather than choosing to engage in the trench warfare of striving for a priesthood of Marian virtue, some seem to have settled for a sterilized and more comfortable lifestyle as their priesthood's truest identity fades."[54]

What a number of Mariologists, theologians, spiritual writers, and authors have acknowledged about the moment of sacred entrustment, when at Calvary Jesus entrusted His Mother to John the beloved disciple, is the fact that John was one of Christ's first priests. This is important, as the priesthood being instituted with the Eucharist during the Last Supper gives the entrustment more

---

[53] Fulton J. Sheen, *The Priest Is Not His Own* (San Francisco, CA: Ignatius Press, 2004), 232.

[54] Wells, *The Priests We Need*, 110.

meaning. In his book *Mary and the Priestly Ministry*, Fr. Emile Neubert explains that it was for a reason that Christ confided His Mother to John. "That is because John was a priest and it is to priests, above all, that Christ gives His Mother because He has a greater love for them and they have a greater need of her."[55] Fr. Neubert poignantly concludes, "Would that all priests would appreciate the implication of this and, like John, take Mary into their lives."[56] In other words, Jesus at Calvary, in the sacred entrustment, was telling generations and centuries of His priests to come that they need to take His Mother into their home, into the interior regions of their soul, to protect and cherish and to allow her to influence and cultivate their spiritual lives.

Scholars usually point to the Gospel of Luke as being the most Marian gospel, since it has the most biographical details about Our Lady's life. Mystics, interestingly, point to the Gospel of John as being the most Marian gospel, since—in their revelations—they show how John took Mary into his home and how she became his spiritual teacher, cultivating his understanding of Christ and his life of prayer and contemplation; his gospel reflects her wisdom, she who knew Christ best. In this relationship, John represents what a priest needs to be: deeply Marian, united with Our Lady.

Renewal in the Church and of the priesthood will not come from more synods, committees, and endless ecclesial discussions, but from personal holiness. The heart of the problem exists not because of a lack of structural reform in the Church—that is a secondary issue, at best—but because of a lack of saints. We need men who are in love with the Eucharist and with Mother Mary, who spend hours in prayer each day, who fast for their flock, who are not afraid to preach truth in season and out of season, who

---

[55] Fr. Emile Neubert, S.M., *Mary and the Priestly Ministry* (New Bedford, MA: Academy of the Immaculate, 2009), 14.

[56] Neubert, *Mary and the Priestly Ministry*, 14.

are not afraid of the Holy Spirit and His gifts and operating in the charisms, who heroically make the effort to overcome temptations and live penitential and austere lives of sacrifice, who desire to grow deeply in their prayer lives to increase their intimacy with Jesus and beloved Mary, an intimacy that is called to become mystical in its interior depths.

Kevin Wells explains the powerful manner in which Msgr. John Esseff understands his relationship with Mother Mary, especially in the midst of struggles and hardships. Wells admits that "after Msgr. Esseff shared this simple understanding of Mary, I have never considered her the same."[57] According to Msgr. Esseff, "Mary is relentless with me":

> "Here's how I picture her: I see her on the ground taking me into her arms at the Fourth Station, and I'm already completely beat and broken." He paused as his voice broke and tears began to well up in his eyes. "And she looks at me and says, 'Your Father said, "You go and die." You better do that, son—you undo it. Please undo this now.' And she helps me up so I can move forward with the cross. That's who Mary is to my priesthood." His tears fell. "I can't be a priest without *this* relationship with Mary."[58]

This relentless, single-minded devotion to the mission of Christ encapsulates who Our Lady is at her core. There is, alongside her tenderness, a toughness in her soul, based on a fierce love of her Lord, pointing to a radical loyalty. That toughness is seen in numerous ways, perhaps most efficaciously in the reaction that evil has to her. Msgr. Esseff, in his life as a priest, has performed countless exorcisms throughout the years. He has repeatedly

---

57 Wells, *The Priests We Need*, 102.
58 Wells, *The Priests We Need*, 102.

witnessed, Wells explains, "demons revealing startling reactions, often horror, at the immensity of Mary's power."[59] Due to this holy assistance and supernatural power of the Woman clothed with the Sun, thus clothed with the power of Christ, he has relied on her to guide his entire ministry against evil in the spiritual battle. We priests are called to do the same.

---

[59] Wells, *The Priests We Need*, 102.

Chapter 8

SACRED INHERITANCE
Embracing the Gift

Behold, your mother. —John 19:27

Mary's motherhood, which becomes man's inheritance, is a gift: a gift which Christ himself makes personally to every individual.
                                        —Pope St. John Paul II

W hy should I pray or talk to Mary?" A common critical question is often asked, tailed by the follow-up: "Why can't I just go directly to Jesus, pray to Him? Why do I *need* Mary?"

There is a deep sadness that underscores this question. The sadness is present in the sense that what a person is essentially saying is "Why do I have to talk to my mother? Why do I need her?"

The question itself is wrongly formulated, as it is not a matter of necessity. Certainly, one can directly speak to Jesus and does not technically *need* to speak to Mary, but it is a matter of divine disposition or pleasure, of what God wills and would satisfy Him. In this case, it is God's will that we pray to Mother Mary. And that is the answer to the question of *why*. Because it is God's will and, therefore, the act of devotion toward His Mother makes Jesus happy.

It is not an accident that God has sent Mother Mary to the world through such major apparitions as Guadalupe, Lourdes, Fatima, and others, sending her with her rosary in hand and giving her the important mission of reaching millions of people, through her maternal presence, to bring them back to lives dedicated to Jesus, His Gospel, and His Church.

The fact that God has decided to use her as an instrument in this important way, a way that includes promoting Marian devotion and the Rosary as a means to help millions of souls come to a deeper spirituality, shows how significant she is in His plan, and how praying for her intercession is part of God's will for our spiritual lives. After all, when she arrives at these apparition sites, she does so not through her own undertaking but through the Father's will, who is sending her for a reason with the intention of spreading greater Marian devotion as a means of bringing souls back to God.

In addition to praying to Our Lady as a way of honoring God's will for our lives, praying to Mary is also about *loving her well* for who she is, our tender and beloved Mother. God has given us a family, a spiritual family that includes countless brothers and sisters in the multiple personalities that make up the Communion of Saints, who intercede for us and (in special ways) enter our lives. Among this family, He has given us a mother. She, this Spiritual Mother, is a special gift that the people of the Old Covenant, the Israelites, did not have. We Christians have the privilege of receiving this sacred gift, this sacred inheritance from Jesus that is an intimate relationship with His Mother, that is the person of Mary.

It was His final act from the Cross, the last task that Jesus wanted to accomplish before leaving for Heaven. He wanted to entrust His Church with a Spiritual Mother. He was not going to leave His Church orphaned. Even before the Holy Spirit descended at Pentecost, Jesus said to the Church, represented by John the beloved disciple, who is a symbol for all beloved disciples, "Behold, your mother" (John 19:27). It is this sacred moment that

Church tradition, in her magisterial writings, acknowledges as the moment when Our Lady officially received her mission and investiture (so to speak) as our Spiritual Mother, a type of painful crowning from the Cross: as she was watching the death of her child, she received special responsibility and sacred authority over the lives of innumerable children, those who were present and those who would come in subsequent generations and centuries.

This reality is depicted strongly in Scripture. In the Book of Revelation, the spiritual warfare is depicted, but in the midst of it, so is Mother Mary's spiritual maternity. "Then the dragon was angry with the woman, and went off to make war on the rest of her offspring, on those who keep the commandments of God and bear testimony to Jesus" (Rev 12:17). Her spiritual maternity begins with the Incarnation. When she said yes to giving birth to the Messiah, the Head of the Mystical Body that is the Church, she became the Mother of the Church.

Likewise, the entrustment that happens from the Cross is multilayered. First, there is the literal reality of John taking Mary into his home, which (incidentally) also constitutes an event that ensures the integrity of Our Lady's virginity—as, by Jewish law, if Jesus had biological brothers, His mother would have to be entrusted to them; the entrustment to John shows that there were no other siblings, the passages in Scripture that reference Jesus's "brothers" pertain to a popular manner, in Semitic cultures, of addressing close relatives, such as cousins.

Second, there is the ecclesial reality of the official entrustment constituting the moment that Christ, as head of the Church, makes His Mother the Spiritual Mother of humanity. This sacred act extended to not only the years that she had left on earth—for Mother Mary to help guide the early Church—but beyond, as an unbroken mission that continues to bear much fruit even after her Assumption into heaven. As the Council Fathers at Vatican II articulated:

Wherefore she is our mother in the order of grace. This maternity of Mary in the order of grace began with the consent which she gave in faith at the Annunciation and which she sustained without wavering beneath the cross, and lasts until the eternal fulfillment of all the elect. Taken up to heaven she did not lay aside this salvific duty, but by her constant intercession continued to bring us the gifts of eternal salvation. By her maternal charity, she cares for the brethren of her Son, who still journey on earth surrounded by dangers and cultics, until they are led into the happiness of their true home.[1]

And third, there is a personal, spiritual reality that Our Lady's entrustment as our Spiritual Mother bears, one pertaining to our interior lives as Christians. In his great Marian encyclical *Redemptoris Mater*, Pope St. John Paul II made a powerful observation, a linguistic nuance that speaks volumes to the interior life that we are called to with Our Lady. He noticed that, in the Gospel passage of John 19:27, which articulates about the beloved disciple, "And from that hour the disciple took her to his own home" (John 19:27), the original Greek has a much deeper and spiritually richer meaning. The great Polish pope wrote, "Entrusting himself to Mary in a filial manner, the Christian, like the Apostle John, 'welcomes' the Mother of Christ 'into his own home' and brings her into everything that makes up his inner life, that is to say into his human and Christian 'I': he 'took her to his own home.'"[2]

This is a profound point. What it means is that to take her into one's own home—which as beloved disciples, like John, we are called to do—necessitates taking Mother Mary into one's interior life, inviting her into one's spiritual life. The Christian

---

[1] Second Vatican Council, Dogmatic Constitution on the Church *Lumen Gentium* (1964), §§61–62.

[2] John Paul II, Encyclical Letter *Redemptoris Mater* (1987), §45.

disciple has a responsibility, as Pope St. John Paul II emphasized, of bringing her "into everything that makes up his inner life."
Fr. René Laurentin emphasizes that after the Apostle John "many
followers since then have taken Mary into their homes. In some
sense, she lives with them."[3]

Relating to Her as a Woman

Another common objection, perhaps more of a struggle than an
objection, that one hears against Marian devotion stems frequently
from female devotees. The objection arises out of a place of insecurity through the (too often repeated) vice of comparison. As a
spiritual director and confessor who has encountered countless
souls and their personal struggles, I know that there is a tendency
among many females to struggle with comparison, and for many
males that similar vice exists in the form of competitiveness.

Here the struggle with comparison is often placed against
Mother Mary. Working at a Catholic university, I have met a
number of devout young women who, although faithful Catholics,
have had difficulties saying Yes to a relationship with the Blessed
Virgin Mary because they see her as representing a feminine ideal,
in her lofty holiness and immaculate purity, that is beyond reach.
In her sinlessness, she is so perfect that it makes her unapproach-
able and unrelatable, the argument goes, especially to any woman
who knows that she can never live up or compare to such heights
of holiness.

This mentality is an obvious block to cultivating a meaningful
relationship with Our Lady. I have met young women, however,
who in their spiritual growth and development have overcome
this mentality. Overcoming it means realizing, foremost, that one
needs to stop the comparison game and start perceiving Mother

---

[3] René Laurentin, *Mary in Scripture, Liturgy, and the Catholic Tradition*, trans.
Sean O'Neill (Mahwah, NJ: Paulist Press, 2014), 74.

Mary for who she is in the relationship: a loving mother. She is a caring, tender mother who loves her daughters immensely and throughout their lives is interceding for them, and not someone to feel threatened by through an unhealthy, and irrational, game of comparison.

I say "irrational" because both Jesus and Mary were conceived and born without original sin, meaning they would not suffer from such effects of sin like concupiscence, that interior struggle between the passions and reason that inclines a person toward sin. Jesus and Mary would possess instead perfect integrity, that is, a perfect harmony in the soul between their passions and their reason. Since the rest of us human beings are touched by the original sin (which is cleansed at baptism but whose effects remain) and therefore have to struggle with concupiscence, we will have tension between our passions and our reason and be more inclined toward struggles that Jesus and Mary, through the sublime dignity of their sinless souls, would not have. This is why comparison is irrational: because there is a world of difference, a different ontological reality, between a regular human soul and a soul that is (through a singular privilege) immaculately conceived. Comparison will always fail and may even reveal a type of subtle pride that is fueled by insecurity—the insecurity of needing to compare oneself.

Now, certainly, as Christians, we are called in our spiritual journeys and development to become more "Christlike," and hence, in that growth we look to learn from the virtues and attributes of Jesus and of His mother Mary, who is the greatest example and reflection of a Christlike disciple. That's a healthy approach. It is an approach that wants to learn personal growth in holiness from the examples and virtues of Jesus and Mary instead of seeing them, in a spiritually immature way, as a threat or competition.

What is also incredibly important to understand, especially if you are a woman or a girl, is the reality that a part of who Mary is, is intrinsically present in you.

What do I mean by this?

There is a theological concept, strongly rooted in the Thomistic tradition, known as exemplary cause. What this concept means is that there is always a preexisting model or pattern upon which something (or someone) in creation is based. In other words, God, in His intelligence and Divine Plan, used a pattern or model, consisting of ideas present in His mind from all eternity, to create beautiful creatures and things. Because Mary was the ultimate model of a woman, being God's perfect creature in the form of a woman, that means she has existed in His mind from all eternity and God has used the model of Mary as a spiritual, moral, and aesthetical image in creating every other woman that has ever lived and that will ever live. That is, every woman created has some virtue, attribute, expression of beauty, that is a reflection of the Virgin Mary, a reflection of each woman's authentic Spiritual Mother.

Chapter 8 of the Book of Proverbs speaks of the personification of wisdom in a feminine figure who was with God before anything else was created and, in fact, was in His presence while He was creating. It was common for medieval theologians to interpret the wisdom literature of the Old Testament and books like the Song of Songs through a Marian lens, seeing Our Lady in the feminine figure in whom God delighted and found inspiration, even in guiding the creative process:[4]

> The LORD created me at the beginning of his work,
>   the first of his acts of old.

---

[4] The excellent work of the University of Chicago historian Rachel Fulton Brown has explored both medieval exegesis of Old Testament texts through a Marian understanding and medieval devotion to the Blessed Virgin Mary. See Rachel Fulton Brown, *From Judgment to Passion: Devotion to Christ and the Virgin Mary, 800–1200* (New York: Columbia University Press, 2002), and *Mary and the Art of Prayer: The Hours of the Virgin in Medieval Christian Life and Thought* (New York: Columbia University Press, 2017).

Ages ago I was set up,
    at the first, before the beginning of the earth. . . .

When he established the heavens, I was there,
    when he drew a circle on the face of the deep,
when he made firm the skies above,
    when he established the fountains of the deep,
when he assigned to the sea its limit,
    so that the waters might not transgress his
        command,
when he marked out the foundations of the earth,
    then I was beside him, like a master workman;
and I was daily his delight,
    rejoicing before him always,
rejoicing in his inhabited world
    and delighting in the sons of men.
(Prov 8:22–23, 27–31)

"Because she is what God wanted us all to be, she speaks of herself as the Eternal blueprint in the Mind of God, the one whom God loved before she was a creature," Bishop Fulton Sheen explains. "She is even pictured as being with Him not only at creation but also before creation. She existed in the Divine Mind as an Eternal Thought before there were any mothers. She is the Mother of mothers—she is the world's first love."[5]

Fr. Stefano Manelli articulates a similar idea in relation to the women of the Old Testament. Even though, historically, Mary was born centuries after the female figures of the Old Testament, in a sense she predated them by being the perfect feminine model that the Lord used, contemplating her in His mind, when creating each woman of ancient Israelite history:

---

[5] Bishop Fulton Sheen, *The World's First Love* (San Francisco, CA: Ignatius, 1996), 17.

In the Old Testament, Mary has been prefigured, as well as foretold and prophesied. In the pages of the Old Testament it is not, in fact, infrequent to encounter in female figures, virgins, wives, mothers, and widows, who typify the Blessed Virgin Mary in one way or another in this or in that virtue. From the totality of all these images one can effectively form a stupendous mosaic of the person and mission of Mary. Here one may verify the reality of that adage according to which what all other women share only partially, Mary instead has entirely in every way and throughout all.[6]

A poignant paradox is found here, and I especially want to address female readers with it. Although for many women Mother Mary may seem like a distant and unrelatable figure, with whom there is struggle to form a relationship because of her holiness and perfection—in her perfection she seems unrelatable to you—it is, actually, in her perfection that she is directly related to you, dear daughter of God, because a part of her exists within you and was used to create you. What a profound reality!

If Our Lady was used as a spiritual, moral, and aesthetical model, so to speak (a "blueprint," as Bishop Sheen would say) by the Divine Artist through whom He sculpted and created every other daughter of His, that means that there is some expression of Our Lady's virtue, goodness, and beauty which exists within every woman, and so there is a direct relatable-ness, as every woman possesses, in one way or another, a quality of feminine beauty that is a reflection of her Spiritual Mother. An image is a reflection of the original; herein every woman is, in some way, a reflection of the Mother of Christ. It is to the point that Bishop

---

6   Fr. Stefano Manelli, F.I., "The Mystery of the Blessed Virgin Mary in the Old Testament," in *Mariology: A Guide for Priests, Deacons, Seminarians, and Consecrated Persons*, ed. Mark Miravalle (Goleta, CA: Seat of Wisdom Books, 2007), 26.

Sheen can write, "She is the one whom every man loves when he loves a woman—whether he knows it or not."[7]

It is easy to miss just how deep and universal this interior union and connectiveness to Mary the feminine genius has. Because, when we say that she is the model through whom each daughter of God was created, we are saying that even the most universal desires and qualities of what it means to be a woman, of the feminine condition, are rooted in her. Bishop Sheen explains the matter with poetic beauty, enunciating: "She is the secret desire every woman has to be honored and fostered; she is the way every woman wants to command respect and love because of the beauty of her goodness of body and soul. And this blueprint love, whom God loved before the world was made, this Dream Woman before women were, is the one of whom every heart can say in its depth of depths: 'She is the woman I love!'"[8]

Relating to Her Sorrow

If a woman, or any person for that matter, perceives Our Lady as unrelatable because of the depths of holiness that she exemplifies, it is important to break this perception by also turning to the life events and experiences of Mother Mary's life that make her deeply relatable. Here it is especially useful to emphasize her experiences and identity as Mother of Sorrows. This is vital to highlight because every human being in the world knows suffering, and, at the foot of the Cross, she experienced the deepest form of suffering imaginable.

Therefore, even if you feel that you cannot relate to her in the realm of virtue and sin—she is sinless while you are a sinner—you certainly can relate to her in the realm of suffering. You have suffered in your life, and Our Lady has suffered immensely. She

---

[7] Sheen, *World's First Love*, 24.

[8] Sheen, *World's First Love*, 24.

understands what it means to go through emotional and spiritual trauma of the greatest gravity, and she invites you to the foot of the Cross to suffer with her. She will hold you, console you through the pain, and offer up those sufferings to her Son, Jesus, for great merits while embracing you with her maternal care and caresses. She knows what it means to suffer the most unspeakable tragedies, a mother seeing her precious child unmercifully tortured, forsaken, and murdered in front of her. Oh, yes, the depths that this tender soul has had to suffer allow her a compassion and empathy that, complementing the benevolent dignity of her soul, is unmatched.

It is because her heart is pierced that she is able to love with such sensitivity, the suffering expanding the interior grace of maternal affection.

Go to her. Do not make the mistake of feeling threatened by her, or of unhealthily comparing yourself to her, unless you're doing so in a manner that is well intentioned because it is desiring personal spiritual growth—a healthy comparison would ask the questions, "Where do I need to grow? What can I learn from her beautiful virtues and attributes? How can my Mother teach me?"

And remember, although she was given the singular privileges of being the Immaculate Conception, Perpetual Virgin, Mother of God, and the one who would be Assumed into heaven, she was still a human creature, a human being who had to face immense trials, difficulties, the pains of misunderstandings being leveled against her Son and herself, periods of profound sorrow and darkness in her life. She understands pain and suffering too well. Because of that, she is also Mother of Good Counsel and Our Lady of Perpetual Help, she who desires to enter our darkness with her maternal embrace, holding us in her arms and gently shedding tears with us in the midst of life's difficult moments.

Fr. Laurentin explains that, when living out a spirituality of the presence of Mary, we cannot ignore the fact that this "presence includes periods of darkness, which must not be overlooked. . . .

It will therefore be necessary to distinguish the reality of the relationship with Mary and the feeling of her presence in the hazards of awareness and sensitivity, especially in the night of faith."[9] This is an essential distinction, as what he means is that Our Lady is also present to us in periods of desolation and darkness, even though her presence in such periods is *not felt*. Thus do we need to distinguish between the relationship with her and a sensitive awareness or feeling of her presence. Here the virtue of faith is especially important, as we may not feel her presence by our side when we are suffering desolating darkness interiorly, but we still need to (one could argue that, in such a case, we especially need to) have faith that she is there when we call upon her assistance, help, and strength.

Fr. Laurentin expounds on this theme, further clarifying how important the presence of the Blessed Virgin Mary is during the darkest nights of trial:

> She is the Virgin of the dark night of the soul. She has been called "Star of the Sea" since the Middle Ages—Our Lady of the *Stabat Mater*, the painful icon of Golgotha, playing her role in these painful transitions, trials, and crosses. In these times of desolation and darkness, death and darkness are not eliminated. She herself has lived through them in faith, but she brings us peace in the cross and in the night. Let us think of her when we are overwhelmed by events and by our own internal difficulties, in sickness or "at the hour of our death," as we say in the Hail Mary. She aims to assist us in our daily trials and the ultimate test of life. She is our mother at the hour of our birth into heaven.[10]

---

9 Laurentin, *Mary in Scripture*, 135.
10 Laurentin, *Mary in Scripture*, 165–66.

To practice a presence of Mary spirituality, therefore, requires turning to her not only as a consoling form of meditative prayer but also in the midst of the storms of life, for, with her maternal love, she desires to be there to help us face those difficulties and trials. It is in those moments when we truly need to speak to her, calling out from the depths of our hearts, "Mother! Please help me. Please come to me. Hold me in this pain."

Being a tender mother who cares immensely about our sufferings, who herself has suffered incredibly and therefore understands our pains and sorrows, she will not say no to the invitation. Even when we do not hear her, she hears us and is lovingly interceding before God for us, being truly present.

Surrendering to Tender Love

We observed in a previous chapter the apparitions of Our Lady of Fatima and how they led to the popular First Five Saturdays devotion, based on the visionary experience that Sister Lucia dos Santos received years later in the convent wherein Our Lady appeared to her with the Child Jesus. As you'll recall, Our Lady was presenting her Immaculate Heart, explaining that it is being pierced at every moment by ungrateful men, and asking for acts of reparation to console her heart. One question that Sister Lucia was faced with, from her confessor, after this mystical experience was: Why did Our Lady ask for *five* consecutive monthly Saturdays when reparation was to be made? In other words, why not *seven* Saturdays or another, more biblical or theologically significant number?

Sister Lucia took the question to prayer and, in 1930, the Lord revealed an answer to her. The request was given for five Saturdays in order to make reparation for the five following offenses:

1. For blasphemies against the
   Immaculate Conception.

2. For blasphemies against Mary's virginity.

3. For blasphemies against the divine maternity
   and spiritual motherhood of Mary.

4. For those who publicly implant in
   children's hearts indifference, contempt,
   and even hatred against Mary.

5. For those who directly insult her sacred images.[11]

The first three offenses here pertain to blasphemies against Marian dogmas and the doctrine of Our Lady's spiritual motherhood. A question may arise: Why does it matter if someone does or does not believe in a Marian dogma, like the Immaculate Conception or Perpetual Virginity?

The reality is that these solemnly defined truths that we call dogmas are not just intellectual abstractions, the cerebral musings of ecclesiastics and theologians, but personal attributes and deep-seated qualities of the Virgin Mary that speak to the dignity of her soul, the integrity of her person, and her moral and spiritual character. That is to say, to deny them is to attack her personhood, her spiritual integrity, and her moral character. It is the equivalent of spreading or believing false rumors against a public figure's reputation; this act becomes slanderous. When it is done against a sacred figure, it becomes blasphemous.

And what is the saddest reality?

That the blasphemy is committed by children against their mother, a mother who loves them unconditionally, has suffered for them, and prays for them ceaselessly. Her love is returned with ingratitude and malice. How can she not be sorrowful?

---

[11] See Jean M. Heimann, *Fatima: The Apparition That Changed the World* (Charlotte, NC: TAN Books, 2017), 72.

Before considering the fourth offense on the list, which deserves greater commentary, let us look at the fifth. The fifth offense speaks of making reparation for those who directly insult Our Lady's sacred images. This horrible sin can be seen in numerous manifestations, from personal sins against her images to public displays of "modern art" which attempt to be deliberately provocative and insulting toward our Holy Mother. It is seen in various expressions of mainstream media which have been on the rise in recent years, from blasphemous films about Our Lady and her apparitions to provocative TV shows and plays meant to mock and scandalize her image, especially her purity. At the heart of it, these are satanic attempts. She has conquered him, and the fact that it is a humble woman, a human creature in her immaculate purity and elevation through grace, who defeats the devil, he who was the brightest of all angels at one point, is a humiliation to him. Hence, the devil rages, and he uses spiritually weak and susceptible souls to enforce his rage through such means.

Notice how this act of reparation calls for making reparation for *those* who insult her sacred images. That is, Our Lord and Our Lady are still concerned about *those* souls; they still love them and desire their conversion of heart and salvation, whereas Satan, who is using them, desires their damnation. We see here the greatness of God's Divine Mercy and the depths of Jesus's cry amidst the horrors of the Cross, "Father, forgive them; for they know not what they do" (Luke 23:34).

Such holy behavior is humility personified. How easily do we get offended over the smallest insult? And yet the Son of God, being crucified and killed, prays to the Father for His tormentors, imploring forgiveness and mercy. The Mother of God, in her sublime dignity, who deserves the utmost veneration as Jesus's mother and Queen of the universe, has her images insulted, and yet she weeps and prays for her children ceaselessly. How wondrous and magnanimous is the example of Jesus and Mary. The word *magnanimity* speaks to greatness of soul, and it is from them that we learn what it means to live magnanimously, choosing mercy over vengeance, choosing light over darkness, including the interior darkness that can enter the human heart, which can become deeply wounded from enduring so much suffering and injustice; not to live in that bitterness, but to transcend. Jesus and Mary teach us the path through the painful but illustrious witness of their lives.

If you are reading this book, you are, more than likely, a person who does not insult Our Lady's sacred images but who is called to make reparation and intercession for those who do. You are also, more than likely, a person who believes in the dogmas and doctrines of the Church, including the great Marian dogmas, and therefore the list of offenses that constitute the five major blasphemies against Our Lady, which Sister Lucia was shown, may not personally apply to you—that is, as anything that you are guilty of. We, devout Catholics, may think this is the case.

But that's not exactly true.

This is where the fourth blasphemy, as listed in Sister Lucia's revelation, comes in. It is one that a number of devout Catholics can still be guilty of and that calls for deeper self-examination and humble spiritual growth. At first, on the surface, the language may not look like anything that a faithful Catholic would be culpable of. But there is a nuance that must not be overlooked. Consider the fourth blasphemy, that we are called to make reparation for "those who publicly implant in children's hearts indifference, contempt, and even hatred against Mary."

Now, for a devout Catholic, implanting contempt and hatred for Mary is usually (if not universally!) not an issue. Hatred and contempt toward Our Lady, tragically, do exist. Often such ideas are implanted in children's hearts through certain sects and denominations of our separated brethren in Protestant circles, who do not have a good understanding of Our Lady's role in Catholic veneration, biblical theology, and salvation history. Therefore, whereas the Bible teaches, quoting Mary, that "all generations shall call me blessed," many Protestant brethren do not refer to her (or treat her with the due honor) as the *Blessed* Virgin Mary, which all generations are biblically taught to do. Whereas the Bible teaches that she is the Mother of God—"And why is this granted me, that the mother of my Lord should come to me?" (Luke 1:43)—and, as we established in previous chapters, the Ark of the Covenant and the Immaculate Conception—"Hail, full of grace" (Luke 1:28)—many Protestant brethren do not show the due reverence that these biblical teachings deserve. Instead, in certain circles a contempt "and even hatred" is cultivated, disrespecting not only the Virgin Mary but also the Word of God, the biblical teachings about her. For such brethren, and for such blasphemies against the Immaculate Heart, we are certainly called to make reparation.

However, where do we, devout Catholics, need to be careful and potentially become more self-aware and reflective when it comes to this fourth blasphemy?

It is in the realm of indifference. The language speaks also— in fact, firstly—about making reparation for those who "implant in children's hearts indifference . . . against Mary." Indifference can be expressed and passed on to children in a number of ways. A major way that it is expressed is by treating Marian devotion as if it is optional, or by equating Marian spirituality with other expressions of Catholic spirituality (and, therefore, reducing it).

What do I mean by this?

Consider the reality that people within the Church have different spiritualities. This is, of course, perfectly true. Human persons are complex, multidimensional beings with different psychological makeups, personality types, and spiritual dispositions. There are a number of different spiritualities under the umbrella of Catholic orthodoxy that are valid expressions of pursuing intimacy with God in the Church. Ignatian spirituality, Benedictine spirituality, Franciscan spirituality, Dominican spirituality, and so on.

But consider if someone takes this point further in relation to the Virgin Mary and, pointing to a group of Catholics, says something along the lines of "People have different spiritualities. He is very Franciscan. She is very Dominican. That one is very Benedictine. And the one over there is very Marian. And that is all good and acceptable, not everyone is the same."

What just happened here?

Notice how Our Lady and her importance became *equated* with St. Francis, St. Dominic, and St. Benedict. Notice also how devotion to Our Lady became *reduced to an optional spirituality*—devotion to her is for *some people*, those who have an inclination toward Marian spirituality, according to this reasoning. This type of reasoning leads to indifference toward our Spiritual Mother and the veneration that she deserves. And it may even happen in the mind of a devout Catholic who treats Mother Mary as if a relationship with her could be optional, as if she doesn't have a uniquely essential role in the spiritual and liturgical life of the Catholic faith but can be treated as a private devotion.

Consider the first part here. When we equate Marian spirituality with Franciscan, Dominican, Benedictine, or any other expression of Catholic spirituality, we are doing a great disservice to Our Lady and to cultivating proper devotion to her. Not only is it a disservice but it is also a theologically faulty perspective that does not honor her unique status and the different levels of devotion that the Church has, in her wisdom, given us.

There are three major levels of worship and devotion. Stemming from the Greek and Latin, the terms are known as latria, dulia, and hyperdulia. Let us consider these categories.

Latria, or in Greek λατρεία, is an expression that denotes *adoration* as the highest form of worship that is to be given only to God. We worship God, we adore Him as the Creator, Redeemer, and Sanctifier, as the Holy Trinity. There is no form of devotion that is comparable to the worship that is latria, that is the adoration we give to the Divine. It is the highest, most sublime form of worship.

Dulia pertains to the veneration (as opposed to worship) that we offer the saints. We venerate the saints as men and women of holiness who reached levels of excellence in their spiritual and moral lives. We venerate them in a living relationship, in the Communion of Saints, knowing that they stand before the throne of God and are able to intercede for us, able to bring our prayers, intentions, and struggles before the Lord.

Hyperdulia is a unique category of devotion reserved exclusively for Our Lady. It is certainly and substantially below latria, below the worship and adoration that we offer to God alone, as she is His creature while He is the Creator. However, it is a category of devotion that is above the saints, acknowledging the uniqueness of the Blessed Virgin Mary in the order of grace. This uniqueness comes from the special privileges that she has from God. She is the only creature, in the history of the human race, who is the Mother of God, who was (after Adam and Eve) immaculately conceived and full of grace, living a life of perfect obedience to the will of God. She is only person, with Jesus, who never committed a sin, even a venial sin.

She is the one person, in the history of the human race, who has an intrinsic relationship with the hypostatic union, with God becoming man; with the Incarnation. St. Joseph, as the protector of the holy family and foster father of Jesus, certainly had a relationship with the Incarnation, but it was extrinsic. Mary's *fiat* and her sacred flesh were offered as a gift to God to bring Him into the world incarnated and provide Him with a body through which He would redeem the human race. She is the New Eve, the one who cooperated morally and spiritually with Jesus, the New Adam, in a unique way to help Him redeem humanity. She is the Mother of the Church because the Church is the body of Christ, of whom He is the head, and because she is His Mother she also becomes our Mother, that of the mystical body.

She has the most intimate and unique relationship with the Holy Trinity that any human being has ever had. She is the only one who can say that she is the daughter of the Father, the mother of the Son, and the spouse of the Holy Spirit.

She is the Queen Mother who has a special role in heaven, above the angels and saints. Her prayers have a special power and efficacy before the throne of God, above all other saints. This is again based on the principle of preeminence, which we observed when considering the potential stigmata of the Virgin Mary: the reality that, being full of grace, she had more graces than any other saint. The power of one's prayer is proportionate to the grace and love that a person possesses. Her prayer, therefore, before the throne of Christ would be most powerful, and that is why she is the strongest of intercessors, the joy and advocate of the faithful, the terror of demons.

This is why it would be false to equate Marian devotion and spirituality with other expressions of spirituality, equating her with the saints. She is not equal. There is a difference between the devotional categories of dulia and hyperdulia. She is not just another saint, and a relationship with her does not represent just another private devotion. She stands higher, the Queen of the saints and angels, the Spiritual Mother of the human race.

Her spiritual motherhood cannot be reduced to the personal preference of a "private devotion." It is in the deposit of faith, present in public revelation, through Scripture and Tradition, that Our Lady was given to us as a Spiritual Mother for all mankind. Pope St. John Paul II, in *Redemptoris Mater*, makes reference to "the Marian dimension of the life of Christ's disciples."[12] Every disciple of Christ is called to have a Marian dimension in his or her spiritual life, a Marian spirituality—it is an essential part of what it means to be a follower of Christ, to receive the gift that He offered His Church at Calvary.

"Mary's motherhood, which becomes man's inheritance, is a gift: a gift which Christ himself makes personally to every

---

[12] John Paul II, *Redemptoris Mater*, §45.

individual," John Paul II explained. "The Redeemer entrusts Mary to John because he entrusts John to Mary. At the foot of the Cross there begins that special entrusting of humanity to the Mother of Christ, which in the history of the Church has been practiced and expressed in different ways."[13]

What the great pope and saint was acknowledging here is the reality that Mary's spiritual maternity toward her children is a gift, a gift that Jesus, in His love for us, has given us; a gift to be cherished and honored. As a gift from heaven, it is a relationship to be cherished and honored. Let us respond to this gift with our intimacy and devotion. Let us respond to Love with love, eliminating any form of indifference in our hearts with pure affection and gratitude for her.

Fulfilling a Dream

St. John Bosco, the nineteenth-century Italian priest who was well-known for his charitable and educational work with the youth, especially with disadvantaged boys, had a famous visionary dream wherein he saw the pope steering a great ship, representing the Church, in the midst of a horrific storm. In order to try to guide the Church to safety, the Holy Father steered the ship toward two columns. One column was larger than the other but they both contained great importance. On the top of the larger column there was a Eucharistic Host with the title "The Salvation of the Faithful." On the top of the smaller column there was a statue of the Virgin Mary with the title "The Help of Christians." The spiritual wisdom of the dream led St. John Bosco to express about the Church, "Only two means are left to save her amidst the confusion: Devotion to Mary Most Holy and frequent Communion."[14]

---

[13] John Paul II, *Redemptoris Mater*, §45.

[14] Brian Kranick, "The Snake and the Rosary: The Dreams of St. John Bosco,"

Similarly, another spiritual leader of our time, Cardinal Robert Sarah, articulated that if "we want to grow and be filled with the love of God, it is necessary to plant our life firmly on three great realities: the Cross, the Host, and the Virgin: *crux, hostia, et virgo.* . . . These are three mysteries that God gave to the world in order to structure, fructify, and sanctify our interior life and to lead us to Jesus. These three mysteries are to be contemplated in silence."[15]

Our Church today is deeply wounded. So many scars. Mother Church, the bride of Christ, is bleeding, Her wounds still very fresh with the scars of scandal, confusion, moral ambiguity in leadership, lack of genuine faith in so many of her shepherds and in such a great number amongst the flock. We need to return to a purer Church. We need to return to a Eucharistic and a Marian Church. A Church that adores the Eucharist and prays the Rosary. The Eucharist makes the Church. And Our Lady, Mother of the Eucharist, is also *Mater Ecclesiae*, Mother of the Church, a protectress and guide who brings us to the foot of the Cross to Jesus, to mystical intimacy with the Crucified One.

The Eucharist is a great gift. It is an extension of the Incarnation, meaning, it is an extension of the presence of Jesus from the time that He walked the earth. He did not leave us. He continues to grace us each day with His humble, physical presence in the Sacrament of His Victimhood, and all that He asks of us is faith and adoration, desiring our friendship and intimacy.

Connected to the Eucharist is the Cross. The Cross represents

---

Catholic Exchange, January 31, 2018, https://catholicexchange.com/snake-rosary-dreams-st-john-bosco. For a book documenting the visionary dreams of St. John Bosco, of which the aforementioned article is a review, see *Forty Dreams of St. John Bosco: From St. John Bosco's Biographical Memoirs*, ed. Fr. J. Bacchiarello, S.D.B. (Charlotte, NC: TAN Books, 1996).

[15] Robert Cardinal Sarah with Nicolas Diat, *The Power of Silence: Against the Dictatorship of Noise*, trans. Michael J. Miller (San Francisco: Ignatius Press, 2007), 47–48.

not only the greatest sacrifice of love offered for humanity but also the great call that we all have: to respond to that love. Pope Emeritus Benedict XVI famously said that we are not called to comfort but to greatness. Greatness includes making demanding decisions, daily moral choices that require interior discipline and asceticism, fasting, self-denial, and sacrifice for the reparation of sins, the conversion of sinners, and our own spiritual growth and love of the Lord. It is a call that is not for the faint of heart. Yet, it is a call that is open to all, as each person possesses within them the God-given capacity for greatness, the possibility to become a saint—the greatest calling of life.

Our Lady is a great gift. Her spiritual motherhood, as St. John Paul II emphasized, is a gift given by Christ to each and every person, a sacred inheritance. Each one is a child of Mary, even those who do not know her and those who reject her. How much hurt she must experience as a mother in enduring so much rejection. Sometimes that rejection comes in subtle ways, including from the children who should love her most.

The Immaculate Heart of Mary has suffered enough hurt. The gifts that the Crucified Jesus has given the world have suffered enough rejection. Our sorrowful Mother has wept enough tears. Let us kindly wipe those tears from her beloved face, embrace her with the tender kiss of our prayers and affection, and say yes to the beauty of a relationship with her, living in union and under the protection of our gentle Mother's presence. Let us embrace the Gift that she is.